Travels through Crime and Place

Travels through Crime and Place

Community Building as Crime Control

William DeLeon-Granados

Northeastern University Press
Boston

Northeastern University Press

Copyright 1999 by William DeLeon-Granados

Library of Congress Cataloging-in-Publication Data
DeLeon-Granados, William, 1964–
    Travels through crime and place : community building as crime control / William DeLeon-Granados.
        p. cm.
    Includes bibliographical references and index.
    ISBN 1-55553-420-1 (cloth : alk. paper).—ISBN 1-55553-419-8 (pbk. : alk. paper)
        1. Crime prevention—United States—Citizen participation.
    2. Community development, Urban—United States. I. Title.
    HV7431.D454 2000
    364.4'3'0973—dc21   99-33755

Designed by Joyce C. Weston

Composed in Sabon by Wellington Graphics, Westwood, Massachusetts. Printed and bound by Maple Press, York, Pennsylvania. The paper is Sebago Antique, an acid-free sheet.

Manufactured in the United States of America
03 02 01 00 99   5 4 3 2 1

For my mother, brother, and sisters,
in whose company I found a passion
for justice and accord

Contents

Contents

Acknowledgments

The people who appear in this work, whether in their own name or in an invented one (to protect their privacy), provided more than their stories and, in some cases, even their homes. They became a buffer against the loneliness and grind of my travels and helped me realize how rapidly community and connection can form between strangers. My hope is that their input may help improve community everywhere.

Among those who gave so much during my travels I am particularly grateful to William Wells, Jennie and James Long, Steve and Emily Plesser, Ty and Melissa Wyman, the Boman family, Amy and Phillip Mazzocco, Cherise Fanno, John "Tommy" Taylor, Cajardo Lindsey, Natalie Kroovand, John Garrish, the Desantis family, Alan Mobley, Christopher Zatzick, Stacey Empson, Philip and Bill Bergin, and Thomas Neese; and to Patricia Caswell for the burger run and for believing in my writing.

Over the past few years several mentors have dispensed honesty, wisdom, and encouragement as I have negotiated the treacherous terrain between science and art. They are Gilbert Geis, John Dombrink, Kip Schlegel, Steven Chermak, and Richard Warren Perry. Additionally, Edmund McGarrell, Alexander Weiss, Harold Pepinsky, and Philip Parnell have always taken the time to listen and to provide feedback.

John Woodcock deserves a special note for helping me embrace my voice by welcoming me, the "scientist," into a creative nonfiction writing workshop way back when at Indiana University, Bloomington. Aimee Bender provided friendship and unwavering support for my style, and Bay Anapoul took time away from her own project to do impressive editing on early drafts. Literary agent Jennie

x   McDonald generously offered critiques and advice as I tried to keep a wide audience in mind. Thanks to William Frohlich at Northeastern University Press for appreciating both the style and concept of the book.

In the midst of my writing, Randall Jackson often came to my aid with a basketball in hand and a good workout on his mind. He never tired of reading drafts, offering his printer, and listening. To Doug and Dana Welsh, Bill and Pamela Lindsay, Colleen Reilly, Paul Rader, Mike Ceely, and, yes, Karen Haubensak: your company and support accentuated life itself.

Foreword

One week after returning to Ottawa from the 1998 annual meetings of the American Society of Criminology in Washington, D.C., former Carleton University sociologist Shahid Alvi and I decided to take a break from our work and visit our neighborhood pub. In spite of the cold November weather, we ventured outside and down the street to be with our own, so to speak, where we could exchange views on the current state of crime control and prevention in our community, in Canada, and in the United States. Over a mug, we talked of popular law and order crime-prevention strategies and their effects as we saw them. We set our minds once again to coming up with alternative strategies, ones that would reach out to the wider society. Our conversation was not optimistic. Shortly after this discussion, I received a copy of William DeLeon-Granados's *Travels through Crime and Place: Community Building as Crime Control.*

The time is indeed right for this book. *Travels through Crime and Place* is one of the most practical and innovative contributions to the understanding of crime control that I have ever read. It is "about alternatives"—not only to understanding the dynamics of social conflict, but also to scientific research methods that investigate them and criminal justice policies that attempt to address them. Why do I say this? DeLeon-Granados has traveled to communities of different sizes, permanence, and health in the United States to observe and to ask: "How does this community understand its conflicts? Who is working to stop crime here? How are they doing it?" The author explores well-publicized avenues of community policing and citizen-watch groups, but then probes ever deeper into what makes a cohesive, functioning community. "Is this community brought together through its efforts or more divided along lines of race or age or politics? What still needs to be taken into account?" Police priorities and behavior are part of the solution, but so are urban design, people's attitudes toward the past, their patterns of consumption, even their own awareness of their power to achieve pragmatic solutions.

As it reaches across disciplines, *Travels through Crime and Place* points the way toward a new paradigm for ailing and disheartened neighborhoods. It suggests that a shared set of community values can be reached through exploration, give and take, and, finally, consensus among members. It raises the possibility of indigenous solutions—specific to a time and place, and developed from within the community itself, from its own agenda.

Travels through Crime and Place is also "about alternatives" in the way DeLeon-Granados uses personal narrative to present his observations throughout the book. In an age in which surveys and quantitative data analysis drive the bulk of North American criminological research, the author encourages us to seek a different route, one that takes people's personal experiences seriously. I am extremely impressed by this, and by the time and effort he devoted to talking to people across the United States. I'm sure that, regardless of their political, empirical, or theoretical orientation, many readers will find his storytelling approach to be so compelling that they will consider following in his footsteps.

In my own case, I'm deeply grateful to William DeLeon-Granados for rekindling my optimism and for taking me on a journey toward a new social order, one that promotes building communities. The depression that permeated my afternoon in the pub with Shahid is gone, owing in large part to reading this book. I hope that, you, too, will find it filled with "good news." The good news, as DeLeon-Granados powerfully points out, is that "people stop crime, specifically people who form cohesive, interdependent communities."

There is much more I can and would like to say about this book. However, I don't want to delay your own travels through crime and place. Still, one last comment is in order before you begin your journey through the pages of this book. Be prepared for a reinvigoration of your imagination.

WALTER S. DEKESEREDY
Carleton University
Ottawa, Canada

Travels through Crime and Place

Introduction

To stop a crime, call a community

> We do not shape our policies to the mistaken and
> infantile notions of the man in the street. Our job is not
> to *ask* them what they think but to *tell* them!
> —Ralph Ellison, *Invisible Man*

More than a generation ago and a lifetime in the past, I spent my first seven years in a world quite apart from the one that most children who grow up in contemporary America experience. For a brief time, before booms in real estate, population, and employment changed a small town some fourteen miles north of San Francisco, California, it was as idyllic, safe, and nurturing as Andy Taylor's mythic Mayberry or George Bailey's Bedford Falls. Narrow neighborhood roads ringed a vibrant main street lined with the town hall, police and fire stations, a church, two bars, two small grocery stores, a theater, a restaurant, a boutique or two, a florist, and several other small businesses.

The butcher at the larger of the two grocers always knew to ask, "Two pounds of ground round today?" when some family member approached the counter with our weekly order. We neighborhood kids spent time in the store crouching on the musty wooden floors at the front, amid boxes and displays of candy. We contemplated, inspected, and weighed our purchases under the owner Sam's watchful eye. Sam often recommended one candy over another based on what he knew about each child's tastes and spending ability.

When we were not ogling candy, we kids freely roamed the streets, exploring, observing, and learning. We hiked through creeks and vacant lots. We visited with neighbors and with the weird but

4   harmless-enough hippies who lived in tepees in a large redwood grove one block up from my house. We played hide-and-seek and jailbreak until Mom's familiar call filtered its way from the front stoop across the darkening neighborhoods to find us somewhere, finally tired and hungry but having too much carefree fun to have noticed.

In the mornings, after my sisters and brother went off to school (before I was old enough to attend), I explored the neighborhood on my own, sometimes hanging out with friends and sometimes spending the days with elderly neighbors. I once followed a utility company lineman on his rounds for a week, donning my leather cowboy boots to greet him each morning as he made his way up our block checking telephone pole connections. On other occasions I pedaled my scooter up to a nearby intersection and swaggered out into the middle, where I directed traffic for amused motorists.

When I began walking to school, I was routinely watched by two retired neighbors on the corner as I made my way up the three blocks to the school yard. On my return in the afternoon, a young woman who frequently sat on her porch reading would look up, wave at me, and say, "Hey, Charlie Brown," as she liked to call me. One sister spent many hours next door with a retired schoolteacher who taught her how to bake cookies, paint pictures, and garden. My brother spent most of his time down the block in a tree house with friends. If we dared speak a derogatory remark to town folk or contemplate and carry out some uncivil act, any adult was likely to correct us.

My forays into the intersection to direct traffic were in reverence to a world that deeply respected public-safety personnel and authority. We knew the names of nearly every police officer in town, and the few whom we saw as mean—the Barney Fifes who often followed the book too closely—were favorites at the dunk tank during the town's Fourth of July celebration. At night, the stillness was sometimes broken by a momentary ruckus as the town's firemen, all volunteers, jumped into their turnouts, dashed from their homes, and clumsily raced to the firehouse, their rubber boots making comforting clopping sounds against the pavement.

One particularly difficult winter around Christmastime, my

mother was struggling to make ends meet. She warned us kids that Santa Claus was not always able to visit every house. We were surprised on Christmas morning by a floor full of presents; years later I learned it was the firemen and police officers who had pitched in to buy them. When my mom could not find a baby-sitter for the five of us, her boss let her bring us to her job at the local theater, where we sometimes watched the same movie over and over.

My world was free from even the thought of crime. Everyone I came in contact with either was someone I knew or knew someone I knew. A stranger in this world would draw immediate attention. To us, strangers who offered candy to children were an abstraction known only to the fictional characters who appeared in grainy black-and-white educational films shown at school. My mother spent more time reminding us to respect neighbors than to watch out for molesters. The hippies down the block smoked something we did not know much about, but they never tried to offer any to us. They did, however, always provide us with pistachios, which we thought were the most exotic thing on earth. Gangs, drugs, pimps and prostitutes, child abductions, graffiti, and urban disorder were realities that would enter my world only after I left town.

That town in my past was a buffer against crime and provided support and nurture for my family. It offered close contact and bonding with people in the community, people I deeply respected. I never wanted to harm those people or cause them distress, because I could identify with them. The network in town transmitted norms about cooperation and provided communication about people who needed assistance. If something happened to someone, the town likely would come to know about it and would respond if needed.

Those characteristics that the small town demonstrated are what sociologist Robert Sampson and his colleagues refer to as "collective efficacy" in their recent landmark study based on a survey of Chicago neighborhoods. Neighborhoods rich in collective efficacy are sources for abundant informal social control, mutual trust, and cohesion. They are places where neighbors can depend on one another for help in times of crisis, and where the social capital of residents provides a powerful regulation of behavior. The good news is that *people* stop crime, specifically people who form cohesive,

6 interdependent communities. The police, the courts, tough no-nonsense laws, repressive shame, the threat of severe punishment, even citizens arming themselves to respond to criminal threats—these strategies certainly can work to a certain degree, but imagine how much more cost-effective, less intrusive, and more globally beneficial a reliance on informal community power can be.

People stop crime by forming a community. By this I mean that a cohesive, interdependent community has the potential to stop a great many crimes, from a street mugging to an industrial manufacturer's dumping pollutants in a lake. Think about how remarkable a statement that is, yet how it is completely underestimated in current American crime-control policies. That communities stop crime by being communities is not very glamorous. There are no high-speed pursuits to talk about, no door-battering drug raids to feast on. In today's action-hungry world, where popular crime-control conceptions include SWAT teams who battle gangs that are armed to the teeth, tough cops who must bend the rules to deal with "human scum," and psychic investigators who hunt down serial killers that make Jack the Ripper seem like a Boy Scout, people remain the most efficient and least noxious method to control crime, reduce fear, and limit disorder.

Mark Cladis is a Stanford University legal philosopher who cautiously warns that a "nostalgic pining for the past will not help" deliver the collective efficacy provided by the town of my childhood. Deliverance "must spring from our current situation," Cladis observes. Glamorizing the past may make us unaware of some very sizable contemporary hurdles that stand before efforts to exploit informal social control.

Building community is an activity to which most of us have become somewhat unaccustomed and perhaps even apprehensive. Still, success stories exist. We need not view a discussion on the capacity of communities to respond to problems such as crime as so much intellectual boasting. The truth is more simple. Drawing on community, and all the undefined allure that the word represents, requires us to look toward efforts to create and sustain community building, to insist on becoming aware of its shortcomings, and to celebrate its power. Ultimately, the truth requires us to accept that there are other ways a culture such as ours may wish to regard crime control and justice.

Although community members often can provide the most appropriate response to problems in their own communities, in this book I show how efforts to exploit citizens' informal abilities face numerous, perhaps insurmountable obstacles, especially in low-income communities. Such communities tend to lack the resources and structures needed to maintain long-term community stability. Official crime prevention can swallow up informal community-based responses, can alienate segments of the population, and can chew up police resources by focusing on arrest instead of strategies that can potentially stabilize a community's social ecology. Moreover, sometimes community-based measures work too well. In 1935, the very first effort to structure ecology-based strategies that relied on developing power within communities, known as the Chicago Area Project, dismayed its architects, Clifford Shaw and Henry McKay, when they discovered that neighborhoods charged with formulating justice for juveniles often acted in a more brutal and more capricious manner than the Chicago criminal justice system.

My own experience left me with the uncomfortable realization that, for all its nurturing, bonding, and cooperative spirit, a small town can also turn petty, mean, and downright unlivable for the wrong people. My family eventually became the wrong people. Despite its allure, our small town was a place where I did not see a black human being until sometime late in my seventh year, and when we did "discover" black people, they were the talk of the town. It was a place where we were children of a low-income single mother who was constantly second-guessed on her child-raising skills. It was a town where nasty feuds developed between neighbors, where husbands cheated on wives and wives cheated on husbands. In that town, firemen and cops hosted parties for a select few to whom they showed confiscated pornographic materials and at which they smoked seized marijuana. It was a town that left my family at the mercy of our landlord, who was also a neighbor. When tensions escalated, we were left without a place to live.

We were displaced from that world only to disintegrate further, my mother being unable to care for all five of us kids. We went

8 where we could—some to an aunt, others to family friends—and the horizon grew bleak. Then came something known as the Great Society, and it helped put my family back together. Unlike that sometimes petty and mean small town, the Great Society was a blind world that welcomed all, but in so doing it concentrated its tired and hungry throngs in blighted places in a rapidly changing country. My mother struggled to avoid moving her reunited family from smalltown life to the public housing projects but had to settle for subsidized housing in a nearby suburban tract.

A new governmental program subsidized our rent in a rickety, one-story cottage in a neighborhood far from the city center, located in a failed real estate development that was designed after Venice with its canals and waterways. When it flopped, it became a landscape dotted with cheap, flat-roofed tract housing that flooded in the winter and was linked to the world only through a convenience store a mile away. Another failed development, a shopping mall, sat empty five blocks from our house. In this world, older neighbors took neighborhood kids to the drive-in and provided them with beer and marijuana.

I was nine when I drank my first beer and tried marijuana. As it turned out, we kids were used by a neighbor as a front. He made drug deals after the movie while we sat in his car. If a cop were to stop him, the driver could say he was taking kids home from the movies. Moreover, we were chased from a park one day by a shotgun-toting Hell's Angel because he was angry one of us had teased his seven-year-old daughter when we were playing with her. On another occasion, my brother and a friend wrestled a rifle away from another friend who, after losing a tennis match to one of them, returned to the park to settle the score.

In the evenings, domestic disturbances could be heard from houses up and down the blocks. Homes sat in disrepair. Anger flourished, as did cockroaches. Many of my fifth-grade peers were in Ritalin-induced hazes. One afternoon a classmate riding a motorcycle led sheriff deputies on a high-speed chase. We watched from the school yard and cheered the classmate when he managed to elude the deputies in the open fields near the playground. One night when as teens we played in a vacant lot enjoying an improvised rope swing tied to a large old oak tree, sheriff deputies showed up and ordered us to leave. Someone said the wrong thing, and the deputies proceeded to beat up everyone present. Some older boys fought back. My oldest sister sobbed uncontrollably. The scene was a sad mess. And my pride for the police of my youth became a hideous joke.

≈ o ≈

I imagine a world between the two poles, where the nurturing collective efficacy of my youth need not fall victim to the disorder and decay of the Great Society, but where the accepting, autonomous Great Society can find room to provide cohesive, resilient community frameworks. I am in luck. Our zeitgeist—that is, contemporary America's intellectual, moral, and spiritual climate—hungers for community in a social famine attributable to provincial suburban neighborhoods and selfish personal regard.

For more than a year and a half I have gathered raw material for stories of this unfolding narrative by visiting people across the United States in places with model community-based crime-reduction programs. I have stayed in their homes, eaten from their tables, and tried to get a sense of what effect these programs have had on their day-to-day existence. I have expanded on my personal experiences by gathering with a large network of friends who serve in the ever-expanding criminal justice industrial complex, including police and parole officers and academicians. I have spent time with people who seem only peripherally connected to the crime narrative—a minister and his family in Oregon, a real estate investor in Massachusetts—but who in their work may have gained a better sense of what constitutes crime control than any police officer or judge. I have witnessed a belief in the community as a way to find redemption from sins like crime and urban decay.

The fashionable appeal created by an appetite for the indigenous problem-solving power that is believed to reside in communities now manifests itself in a variety of ways. Through a series of stories I intend to examine some of the more popular manifestations of that appeal. Before I begin, however—that is, before we take this journey together across the community-as-crime-control landscape to map its topography—let me suggest an alternative frame of mind that all travelers would be wise to consider.

This book is about alternatives, about the way crime control is conceptualized, the way scientists go about investigating their subject matter, and the way those investigations are reported. I will describe personal experiences that have particularly powerful meanings. I do this, in part, to provide a framework from which I intend to examine social policy designed to curb crime through the potentially efficacious power indigenous to communities. Science advances in a rather unremarkable but robust fashion, I was told once, when a theory, no matter how well conceived, tested, and supported, fails to jibe with someone's personal experience, because an alternative take or hypothesis is then suggested, examined, and tested, and so goes the tireless march of knowledge.

The process of testing and refining requires gathering data and then subjecting those data to analysis in an attempt to make some assumptions about the world. For instance, I could gather survey responses about how safe people feel in a certain neighborhood that has implemented a community-policing program. I could decide to implement my own community-based strategy and see how it fares based on rates of crime before and after the program went into effect. Such strategies are important, useful, and fairly straightforward components for learning about social phenomena. Yet I have chosen a more arduous route made necessary by my insistence on using a method that best values the stories heard in my travels.

Stories are fast becoming a popular discourse in the social sciences. It is not that they have not always been there, but their validity as hard-and-fast science has always been called into question. Additionally, science seems yet unwilling or perhaps unable to grasp fully, without crutches, the storytelling paradigm. In an entire issue of the *Michigan Law Review* devoted to storytelling, only two submissions use a true storytelling framework, in that the authors do not set out to support and defend their work. Instead most authors trace an outline of the things to come that is so deliberate as to be almost embarrassing to read. The two authors who shun this framework produce novel pieces that leave the reader at first uneasy and unsure. I suspect this is because readers with an eye to science and law have been trained to a certain language and efficiency in reading, just as we have been trained to a certain language and efficiency in the nature of crime control. Students of crime are more likely to be trained in running a statistical computer package than in crafting a coherent, meaningful story. I believe the need for stories linked with analysis is so great that I am willing to live with the rough-cut appearance of my work. I want to use the method to convey its power.

The alternative for me is frustration. I am frustrated by the way I see colleagues dance around concepts like empowerment, community, multiple narratives, and democracy and then lace their discussions with so much jargon and pomp as to make them unintelligible for all but the most indoctrinated readers. I am frustrated because research that seems to make sense by my alternative hypothesis does not succeed on its own merits, because a more effective communicator, or a more politically astute scientist, can better package his or her own ideological mission under the guise of science.

My frustration gives way to resolve. I will demonstrate that building community can develop into a messy prospect, made more so by relying too much on formal, top-down ideas about what it takes to control crime, and not enough on the long, sometimes uneasy road built on stories and narrative, dialogue and communication, trial and error, give and take. I recall the words of Cornel West, a Harvard University professor of religion and Afro-American studies, during observances to mark the Holocaust: "Stories offer a value that science cannot always provide." The key is to situate ourselves in stories and narratives to find something more than ourselves, to find something about our relations with one another, to find our humanity. West suggests that such a process will help divided people connect with one another.

≈ o ≈

If it is ultimately personal experience that makes or breaks a theory, then I will defer to personal experiences discovered in the field to make or break my examination of social policy. The policies I examine are all strategies intended to evoke community power. The stories

I present suggest that the strategies not only poorly serve those aims but also perpetuate dangerous, unhealthy divisions and tensions between race and class groups in communities. That they do so is my alternative hypothesis. I argue that ongoing conceptual ruts that value programmatic inventions over community stability in the prevention of crime control limit the ability of actors such as the police to exploit community problem-solving capabilities. That our current community-based crime-control strategies fail to address even peripherally such issues as domestic violence and white-collar crime, yet may make people feel safer, further suggests to me that they relieve symptoms but do not ease causes.

Make no mistake about it: I am not about to construct an argument that asserts that it is good for a community if gang members coexist alongside law-abiding home owners, prostitutes prowl city streets as children play, drug dealers ply their trade (as long as they do so to adults), and homeless individuals have a right to harass and abuse others. My own personal narrative is at play here. It is a narrative shaped by a sadness that I should see fellow citizens afraid in their own homes and worried in their own neighborhoods. My narrative is also a product of a pulse-pounding fear that sometimes rousts me from sleep at night when a strange noise in the garden helps my imagination conjure the visions a disorderly world conveys.

At the same time, my personal narrative is born of a brutal beating from sheriff deputies hell-bent on restoring some order among unruly teenagers hell-bent on doing some rope swinging. I do not wish to provide an argument that police provide the only means for maintaining order and for constructing community crime control. Although they, like any member of a community, remain an important component, we other members of the community sometimes defer to the formal criminal justice system and forget that the most powerful form of crime control remains in developing healthy, stable, resourceful environments. To the extent that police can serve that agenda, community members should welcome them as players in the community project.

I examine these issues by relying on popularly conceived models of crime suppression, such as community policing, and then mixing in the stories I have heard as they relate to the issues raised by those policies. For instance, in chapter 1 I begin by returning to a world similar to that of my childhood. Mukilteo, a town on the shores of Puget Sound in Washington State, faces unprecedented growth, while the town leadership struggles to find a model for the town's future that will balance that growth with a desire for safety and a satisfactory quality of life. This chapter reflects the struggle faced by community leaders as they attempt to create a community in an environment inhospitable to such a goal.

In chapter 2 I examine community policing, primarily from the perspective of police officers who offer their skills and services to draw on community power. Using the community-policing rubric, today's police officer resembles a market researcher, actor, inspirational speaker, grassroots organizer, educator, and high-powered needs consultant.

In chapter 3 I examine the community's role in partnerships with the police to round up suspected gang members; to form coalitions to watch and report on activities at local crack houses; and to sponsor drug education and drug resistance programs, block watches, school watches, home alerts, and neighborhood watches. Police also now train citizens to patrol neighborhoods and conduct academies at which citizens undergo pared-down law enforcement training programs.

These first three chapters will touch on a theme now making its way into police stations around the world. From the oppressive governmental regime in Singapore to the street democracy of Berkeley, California, community policing shapes police strategy like no other model since Sir Robert Peel professionalized policing by forming the London Metropolitan Police Service in 1829. Despite its immense popularity as a policing style, the original community-policing concept seems missing from most policies. What remains, depending on whom one asks, is a copiously applied but ambiguously conceived model with as many originators as frameworks.

When community policing is discussed, Herman Goldstein, at the University of Wisconsin, and UCLA political scientist James Q. Wilson are most often credited as the fathers of community policing. Although Goldstein and Wilson have indeed been influential police strategists, they have never actually articulated the same fundamental theoretical grounding applied by the late Robert Trojanowicz, a professor and police researcher at Michigan State University. Trojanowicz's community policing is built upon the notion of police acting as catalysts for local change, helping residents exploit their own informal social control abilities. More important, Trojanowicz's model tries to articulate ways in which police can prevent crime by engendering participation by all members of a community, from crime-prone teens to crime-weary senior citizens. The error in ascribing creative origination for the theory may seem trivial, but the truth is that the policing models put forward by each of the aforementioned men differ significantly.

Goldstein's model refers to "problem-oriented policing," a method to create strategies aimed at reducing repeated 911 calls regarding the same location. Using problem-oriented policing, officers have, for instance, sprayed noxious-smelling paint in tunnels frequented by teens to make the sites unappealing as hangouts. While this theory depends on creative problem solving and not solely on arrest, and has shown promise in reducing trouble at locations prone to crime (or "hot spots"), it does not demonstrate an appreciation for the social issues at the root of crime or the informal social mechanisms that reduce a host of social problems such as crime.

Wilson's policing model stems from his seminal articles coauthored with George Kelling, "Broken Windows" and "Making Neighborhoods Safe," which appeared in the *Atlantic* in 1982 and 1989 respectively. Drawing on the work of Philip Zimbardo, a noted social psychologist, Wilson and Kelling illustrated how decay in urban neighborhoods begot further decay. Conversely, repaired windows would induce residents to take a continued stake in the appearance of their neighborhood and make it undesirable for deviants. Wilson and Kelling's approach is best defined as place-oriented and order-maintenance policing. I tackle these ideas in chapters 4 and 5. Chapter 4 also considers incivilities as they relate to crime and explores how they may stem from a lack of shared cultural standards, or shared meanings, about public conduct.

The notion of a lack of shared meaning is important because it can offer an approach to understanding incivilities that is qualitatively different from the approach taken by most problem-oriented policing currently under way. The current process attempts to control incivilities through a variety of policing functions typically using some deterrent or threat. By contrast, when the ambition is to develop shared meanings on public conduct, the process seeks to broaden social relations to the extent that people begin to appreciate and adopt a shared norm of behavior.

"Most police work is concerned, not with serious crime, but with regulating public conduct," Wilson told us in his timelessly influential work *Varieties of Police Behavior.* Wilson's perspective is important because it underlines how order-maintenance and place-oriented crime-control efforts contradict Trojanowicz's community-policing ideas. In fact, Wilson's work, originally published in 1968, used data from police styles in eight American cities specifically to argue against team policing, the precursor to community policing.

What was it about team policing that bothered Wilson? He viewed it as policing by consensus, a model more akin to socialism or policing in Communist China than fit for the political system of the United States. He worried that policing in a democratic fashion, where citizens had more say, jeopardized police authority. Police were most effective when they determined their own goals and style; it was, after all, best to leave the mission of the police to the men in blue (and in 1968 they were mostly men). Only police could effectively determine what evidence pointed toward the need for the intrusive apparatus of the state, and only police could remain free from political influence. Wilson put it this way: "What the proponents of the communal model are, in effect, recommending is that we 'suburbanize' the central city—let each neighborhood (usually defined along class and race) determine its own style of law enforcement. This view of the police is in keeping with the recently acquired opinions of certain liberals and radicals that decentralization and 'participatory democracy' are among the chief remedies for social problems."

No matter how potentially problematic Wilson viewed policing by consensus, an argument could be made that such policing already had taken place in America along color lines. Generally, black

Americans were policed at the behest of white Americans. This cynical image was painfully exposed for all to see more than twenty years after Wilson's thesis, with the 1991 broadcast of Rodney King's beating by LAPD officers. In 1993, law professor Jerome Skolnick and NYPD-officer-turned-university-professor James Fyfe detailed in *Above the Law* the inequitable application of American policing. As Skolnick and Fyfe demonstrated, policing was an act intrinsically linked to interest groups directing state power against the threat du jour. Most often the threat was black, especially young and male, but that was not always the case. In one stark example, the consensus turned against antiabortion advocates in the streets of Los Angeles when a liberal city council member, who previously had been a harsh critic of the LAPD, encouraged the police to come down hard on the protesters.

In the late 1960s, the images created by neighborhood team policing were juxtaposed with images of Communists putting down democratic uprisings in Eastern Europe and relentlessly invading Southeast Asia. Perhaps team policing, though a democratic principle, was too much to swallow for a country embroiled in cold-war rhetoric and fears of worldwide socialism, and threatened by sharing power with radical groups and the young.

Years later, a young Trojanowicz, the son of a beat cop, would take the team-policing concept for a different but evocative spin after he observed how police officers dealt with a troublesome group of teens in a crime-ridden park in Flint, Michigan. Instead of creating a curfew in the park, increasing patrols, spending hours on surveillance, mounting a sting operation, trying to find a way to make the park unattractive for the teens, or driving them off via angry and mobilized residents, the officers Trojanowicz observed put the teens in charge of park maintenance. They armed the group with rakes, brooms, and other maintenance equipment, gave them responsibility for the upkeep of their hangout, and regularly met with them.

There is something inspiring about this tale. It draws to mind the Camelot legend, how King Arthur controlled his knights by sharing his power and respecting their ability to lead and to become viable members at the Round Table. The police officers Trojanowicz observed did not operate on perceptions that today's youths are incorrigible, lack moral guidance, or are downright violent. Instead they gave the youths a place at the community table. The youths must have taken their roles seriously, because vandalism and other incivilities in the park declined even though the officers did not step up patrols. When the officers did visit the park, they always met with the youths, making the patrol visit a community experience.

There is a problem with such a strategy in contemporary America, when most of the public focuses on sins and thinks that the threat of punishment is the key to prevention. The officers in Trojanowicz's account had to look beyond who these youths were, what records they may have had, and what their past transgressions may have been.

A similar program under way in San Francisco puts former gang members on safety patrols in city buses. The program has met as much opposition as it has garnered proponents, because many are uncomfortable with both the risk and the moral statement implied in giving former gang members places of status. When Jesse Jackson called for a national sit-down (a sort of peace talks) with youth gangs in Chicago several years ago, public outrage was so great that Jackson had to change his plans. A Chicago columnist likened the event to sitting down at the bargaining table with the Nazis.

Some policies aimed at drawing on community power and stimulating proactive, informal social control inadvertently keep community members apart, increase alienation in some circles, and fail to help individuals overcome their inability to look beyond past sins. Perhaps policies that do not directly address crime but work to shape community mixing can overcome the hurdles faced by more mainstream crime-control models. In chapter 6 I examine New Urbanism, which comprises efforts to bring communities together through city planning and through encouraging social mixing. Urban planners believe New Urbanism represents an effort to induce people to mix and rub shoulders in hopes that such mingling will develop community.

Chapter 7 reveals how legal scholars see a way to construct community by relying on legal codes and civil processes. Communitarian-based legal theory has given rise to civil cases resulting in laws against neighborhood nuisance houses; laws establishing curfews, driving restrictions for teens, drug tests for employees, mandatory seat belt use for motorists and helmet use for motorcyclists and bicyclists, restrictions on access to the Internet, and parental responsibility for children affiliated with gangs or illegal activity; and laws prohibiting suspected gang members from using cell phones or hanging out together. The question remains, however, whether such laws will help us develop relations with those around us and form that interdependent, connected social world where community power and informal social control naturally flourish.

In current policy grounded in appeals to community, from community policing and order-maintenance policing to New Urbanism and communitarianism, we know some stories, but others we do not know. In those stories that we have failed to come to know, there may exist important themes that can still touch something in us. These themes may offer inspiration and may help provide a better understanding of the role community can play in reducing crime and generating a better quality of life. For instance, in reflecting on the supposed value derived from community policing, I want also to appreciate how it has actually hampered race relations in some neighborhoods. By fully understanding the complexity with which efforts to construct community manifest themselves, in the conclusion of this book I provide a framework to correct deficiencies and to generate more beneficial policies. I apply this framework to several hypothetical community problems and explain how to conceptualize crime control as a product of a cohesive, interdependent, fully connected community.

Reaching that final chapter requires some bravery on the reader's part. We should be brave enough to listen to stories that suggest that efforts to construct community (or to reconstruct the ideal image of the lost community) may not always yield the results we so optimistically seek. Efforts to find that elusive community and to rely on it to foster peace and safety in neighborhoods across America may create other problems, including increased alienation and the formation of wedges between racial groups. A reliance on the community can offer a way to heal racial and class wounds, to help bring people back into the fellowship of a community, and to overcome an over-reliance on formalized criminal justice processes to solve social ills. But we cannot get there until we map where we are going.

1. *Mayberry* versus *Starsky and Hutch*

Leadership striving to form community

Evil deeds are rarely the product of evil people acting
from evil motives, but are the product of good
bureaucrats simply doing their job.
—Social psychologist Philip Zimbardo,
"On Obedience to Authority"

Brian Sullivan is holding court. As the mayor of Mukilteo,
Washington, Sullivan regularly conducts business from his
family-owned brewery on a hill overlooking the city's pictur-
esque waterfront. This morning, a summer before he will leave the
post that he has held for eleven years, Sullivan sits enjoying coffee
with the director of public works and a new streets division hire.
Sullivan's bold, sincere smile and jocular demeanor soften his
marine-style crew cut and former college wrestler's build. With jokes
and compliments he greets the occasional visitor who stops in to say
hello.

He is a mayor whom any big-city resident might covet. He wants
his town to be a model responsive, inclusive, and problem-solving
community, and he wants the police to help build that community.
Sullivan echoes many administrators when he talks about modern
policing and community building: "You don't build community by
being reactive. You do it by being proactive." Being proactive for
Sullivan means being responsive; being responsive is the stuff of
Sullivan legend. A day before I visited Sullivan, the city police chief,
Jon Walters, told me that Sullivan once delivered a dog-license application to the town clerk to ease the concerns of a citizen caught up in
some bureaucratic snafu. The public works director reaches over

and nudges Sullivan to recount the "great snowball incident." On a winter morning not too long ago, a local resident burst into Sullivan's office and beaned Sullivan with a snowball composed of snow and rock salt. Then the resident admonished Sullivan for salting city roads, warning him that the salt would ruin the paint on the resident's new BMW. "He hit me right in the face. After I explained to him how he wouldn't have a BMW if it slid off some icy road, he started to get the picture. These people move up from Seattle and just don't understand what we're trying to do here."

What Mayor Sullivan is trying to do is to maintain the benefits and sanctity his familiar, small-town leadership style allows in a fast-changing world. Mukilteo has become something of a way station. Twenty-four miles to the south lies Seattle. On the town's west edge are the cold waters of Puget Sound and Saratoga Passage. Whidbey Island, a popular tourist destination, sits on the opposite shore. The city exists in two sites: an old town of approximately seven hundred residents—along with an unmistakably quirky seaside attitude—and the twelve thousand or so people who have come in the last six years to live in new developments up the hill south of the old town. Sullivan adamantly believes in responsive government and the power of a cohesive, interdependent community to solve problems. His residents, however, seem happiest when left alone. They are the same residents who voted a few years back to close the public library.

At a town celebration complete with barbecues, game booths, and a parade, the mayor stood on a sidewalk and proudly watched his town put on its best face. As baton-twirling majorettes and fire engines with sirens wailing made their way along the parade route, a blaring car horn disrupted the festive atmosphere. A resident, with boat in tow, was honking because the parade blocked exit from his driveway. The mayor approached the irate driver and politely suggested he should relax, turn off the engine, and enjoy the short parade. The mayor's suggestion seemed only to anger the driver further. He demanded that the mayor momentarily halt the parade so that he could take his boat down to the water. The driver declared that he couldn't care less about the town, that his house was a mere investment, and that his emotional investment did not extent to

Mukilteo's civic affairs. Sullivan, ever the responsive leader, tried to placate the driver until an opening in the parade allowed the driver to leave.

LEADERSHIP AND PARTICIPATORY STYLES

Before Sullivan came into office in 1986 the Mukilteo Police Department was a shabby, dangerously slack outfit operating out of a bankrupt mortuary, which itself was a pieced-together double-walled trailer. The department did not require officers to carry standardized equipment and held them to few rules. "Some guys literally carried cannons and wore torn patches on mismatched uniforms. We hired officers who were fired someplace else, gave them seven dollars an hour, no training, and off they went," laments Sullivan. Some of the officers were known drug dealers. Sullivan set up a town meeting to discuss police department issues and to develop solutions, but the town's abilities were strained and at an all-time low. When one of the corrupt officers walked into the meeting room, other officers stood up and left. Citizens lost faith in the police. Police lost faith in the citizens. The department took on a siege mentality. In one incident, an officer pulled over a well-known local resident for a stop-sign violation and came to the car window with his gun aimed at the head of the driver. The driver did a double take, recognizing the officer as a former high school classmate. The driver took the initiative to establish rapport with the officer and calmed his edgy nerves.

Sullivan's first major change was to hire Jon Walters as police chief. Although Sullivan is pleased with Walters and the changes that have taken place, he remains far from completely satisfied. He candidly cautions that all he did with the department was "jerk it into the twentieth century." He wants something more. Sullivan is hopeful that Walters can deliver that something more, but he knows that Walters's talents make him highly appealing to a big-city department offering more money and more prestige. "I know eventually we'll lose him, but we've got to do what we can while we have him," Sullivan notes.

When he was hired, Walters became the youngest-ever chief of police in the state of Washington. He is sincere, gregarious, and youthful looking. Wearing a polo shirt, stylish glasses, and slacks, he comes across more as a young, upwardly mobile executive in the entertainment or computer industry than as the kind of obstinate, cowboy-booted lawman I am used to seeing. His most appealing quality is that he does not hesitate to admit it when he does not have an answer. He knows that he does not want to rely on arrest as a problem-solving strategy. One day, as we drive by a man loitering on a corner and drinking from a beer can in the middle of the day, Chief Walters bemoans, "You see, that's illegal in the state of Washington," but he does not cite the man. Other cities have discovered an apparent correlation between lower felony rates and the rousting of street people from their corner perches to enforce misdemeanor laws such as loitering and drinking in public, but Walters fails to find comfort in such strategies.

Mukilteo has a police department that solves order problems but is not always focused on making arrests, a mayor who is concerned with modernizing and improving the image of the department, and a chief whose desire is to heed the public's call. Political scientist James Q. Wilson calls a department with these characteristics a "service-style" department. According to Wilson, in communities that host such departments, that is, communities "which are not deeply divided along class and race lines, the police can act as if their task were to estimate the 'market' for police services and to produce a 'product' that meets the demand." Wilson also suggests that men like Sullivan and Walters are able to pursue the service style because the structure of their community allows for it: "This style is often found in homogenous, middle-class communities in which there is a high level of apparent agreement among citizens on the need for and definition of public order but in which there is no administrative demand for a legalistic style." The "legalistic style" exists in communities with more minority and low-income residents, where the officer routinely takes a law enforcement role rather than maintaining order with more informal means. "Almost invariably a legalistic department was once a corrupt or favor-doing department," Wilson says, and it must enforce the laws to appear above suspicion and to avoid class or race conflict. Wilson's thinking is that a legalistic department cannot run the risk of creating discord among various class and ethnic groups. When discord does surface in cities with such departments, Wilson manages to maintain his thesis by arguing that friction is not the result of legalistic departments failing to enforce the law uniformly but is due to behavior differences among citizens: Because "juveniles, Negroes, drunks, and the like . . . are more likely than certain others to commit crimes," Wilson argues, "the law will fall heavily on them and be experienced as 'harassment.'"

Although Sullivan fears losing Walters, Wilson's thesis suggests that Walters's style would not fare well in a more heterogeneous city like Spokane, Washington. As I will explain in the next chapters, places like Spokane face uphill struggles with their community-policing styles. However, Wilson's analysis also overlooks the important variation in the styles of visionary leaders, irrespective of the communities in which they serve. Walters might excel in any community. Combined, Mukilteo's two leaders constitute a powerful resource. They simply refuse to seek comfort in the way things are. They will drag their community, kicking and screaming if need be, toward participatory styles of government.

This top-down interpretation may seem to confuse my analysis, which relies on community-based response and the innate grassroots problem-solving ability of residents. But Walters and Sullivan demonstrate a top-down approach to a bottom-up process only on the surface. Walters defers to the community and relies on a participatory democratic style in a remarkable fashion. He demonstrates a desire for innovation and an anxiety over a lack of clear direction when, several times during my visit, he asks me what I have seen in my travels. He wants to know if I have found any special way to entice citizens toward a world inhabited by interdependent and communicating members of a cohesive community.

Because at first glance Mukilteo residents seem reluctant to join in the vigorous democratic experiment that Walters envisions, the cynic in me suggests that town residents are happy with the way things are and are better left alone. There is little crime in the town, and residents in any town or city do not often develop the motivation to address a nonexistent problem. This means that Walters needs to find another avenue to stimulate citizen input. Should crime patterns change in the town, which he believes will happen because of continued growth, he can then call on the citizens.

The essential problem that Mayor Sullivan and Chief Walters face is that Mukilteo citizens show little interest in implementing traditional community responses to crime, such as Neighborhood Watch or Home Alert. Sullivan and Walters seem generally dismayed over futile efforts to bring people together to build that elusive community; they see the handwriting on the wall. Walters already has to contend with parking violations, loitering teens, and vehicle vandalism on the streets surrounding the new but crowded high school.

Mukilteo residents are able to maintain a comfortable lifestyle and hence are relatively autonomous beings. Perhaps they wish Mukilteo had a service-style department that left them to their own affairs. One resident who formerly held such a view, but is now a police advisory committee member, told me that the people he talks with do want to be part of something larger in the community. However, it is always hard to reestablish relations that have been deadened over time or severed because of bureaucratic insensitivity. He suspects residents find it easier to withdraw than to develop new relations, but once rapport has been established and the momentum builds, residents will start wanting to join the effort: "I have lived in a lot of places, in Fremont [California] and Seattle. I belonged to neighborhood associations in those places and thought they did us just as good as anything else. When you're in those cycles you don't see the need for relations between individual homeowners."

This man tells me that through his work on the advisory committee he has come to understand conflicts between police officers and citizens. The most persistent problem is officers treating citizens with insensitivity. If a driver is stopped for a traffic violation, he or she is sometimes more offended by the citing officer's treatment than by the ticket. "A majority of the citizens want to trust the police," the committee member explains, "but we have to draw the community in, allow candid input, and provide candid exchange. This will build the trust and then it is up to the department to respond to it."

Although it is hard to start dialogue and build community, once the ball is rolling "people enjoy being part of a culture where they can talk to one another," the committee member says. The key need seems to be for the leaders in bureaucratic institutions—who are often seen as supporting cold, uncaring structures—to provide the initial link in developing trust and overcoming inertia to draw in the community. Walters realizes that his assignment as police chief means taking the initiative to overcome sins of the past. He has done this, in part, by welcoming the police advisory committee. He sees events such as ice cream socials, potlucks, and even "cookies and coffee on someone's front lawn" as important tools. Unlike a service department, which is more likely to just keep the lid on order violations, Walters's department looks on every problem, so long as things don't get out of hand, as an opportunity to hone the community's problem-solving skills. A barking dog, a lonely neighbor, bored teens, and neighborhoods that need sprucing up all become important target points in paving the way for more community-based efforts in the long run.

Most problems that Walters typically faces do not conjure nightmarish images. Even so, to Walters, community-oriented policing really means cogoverning with the citizens of his town. He drives me along a residential street to where the pavement drops sharply from a high crest, down out of the neighborhood and into a county road. The neighborhood had complained about the excessive speed of drivers coming down the hill as they edged their accelerators up in preparation for the sparsely populated county road ahead. The drop is sharp enough that a car with sufficient speed could fly off the crest and lose control.

Walters found himself mediating with city traffic engineers, the city council, and the county on behalf of the neighborhood. He organized a meeting with all the parties involved, at which he discovered that his usually responsive city council did not favor speed bumps; nor did the county. When the parties finally agreed on placing speed bumps, a new debate emerged as to where the street crews would locate them. After there was agreement upon a location, Walters realized that a speed bump placed near the crest of the hill actually would make more of a ramp at the top of the hill, only increasing the likelihood that a driver would fly out of control. The parties met again. After considerable dialogue, Walters, the concerned residents, and the city agreed on a solution. The county signed on to the agreement only after the city gave its backing. The result: speed bumps well before the crest of the hill, new street striping, new warning signs, and increased traffic patrol.

In another incident the school district sent flyers to parents warning them about a paroled sex offender living in the city. Other flyers were passed out at school. Sullivan recalls that the flyers created a palpable hysteria. To complicate matters, the paroled offender's brother attended fifth grade in the school district. He saw a flyer with his brother's picture. The incident exposed him to ridicule from other students, and parents began to fear their children's associating with the youngster. The boy became distressed and confused. He failed to grasp the community's anger, especially since his brother was undergoing treatment and trying to abide by his parole agreement.

Walters took the lead. He attended a series of town meetings the purpose of which was not only to voice residents' concerns but also to share stories about the fifth grader and his brother. The neighbors not only were offered suggestions for what they could do to prevent molestation, but they also faced the source of their fear. Walters explained that the offender was sick and troubled, his brother an innocent, and through the discussion and storytelling Walters reintroduced their humanity to the residents. The key for Walters was to prevent hysteria that might lead to vigilantism and might make parents fearful about their children's playing in the neighborhood.

The buck-stops-here attitude was important to Walters, especially if he was to put his ideas of the community as problem-solver to the test and develop informal social control in the community. Sullivan tells me that in a neighboring city, residents burned down the house of a sex offender who previously had been run out of Arizona. He reasons that any community can push its problems out; it takes special leadership and bold community members to attempt to see every problem as one their indigenous skills can address.

Walters voices a refreshing frustration over the endless cycle begun by arrest, which is presented as the only problem-solving tool afforded leaders in his position. He seeks something more powerful, something that most leaders might not yet envision but that they should continue to look for. He sincerely seems at a loss for effective solutions, although he wants to move forward. Federal statistics record crime at its lowest levels since 1973. Everyone who can claim credit has done so, including legislatures that have enacted tougher penalties and police departments that have engaged in innovative anticrime strategies such as community policing and tough enforcement of misdemeanor laws.

Those cities witnessing the largest drops in crime, such as New York, have also seen a rise in citizen complaints to organizations like the American Civil Liberties Union (ACLU). As a result, New York's policing tactics have come under increased scrutiny by the ACLU. The organization believes the new enforcement strategies do much more than just upset minorities, as Wilson indicates they invariably do.

Former San Jose, California, chief of police Joseph McNamara, now a Hoover Institute research fellow, tells *Time* magazine that stepped-up enforcement strategies create an atmosphere that leads to a siege mentality among the police. A disturbing picture of arrest as the problem-solving tool again arises, rooted in the fact that one in four American males has an arrest record, a chilling fact for any democracy.

It may very well be that increasing misdemeanor arrests leads to reduced overall crime. Random searches of kids dressed as gang members might reduce street violence. Billions spent on prison construction and increases in criminal sanctions may deter potential offenders. What all this says about American culture and the way it deals with problems is the question Walters has about these strategies. Walters's concern is well founded when I consider that the security and freedom from fears that most Americans seek never seem to be swayed by drops in crime statistics. The work Walters is doing makes a substantive statement about justice. He knows that, on the one hand, increasing arrests may reduce crime. On the other hand, what value statement does a culture make with that type of crime-reduction tactic, one that still leaves neighbors fearful?

Herein lies the heart of the matter. Walters believes that focusing on the community can offer the same quantifiable crime- and fear-reducing results that other strategies do, and that such a focus relies on a process that is far less noxious, that values human dignity, and that celebrates a knack for innovation. But by trying to rely on his community, Walters knows he faces a difficult challenge. He knows that at the moment few comprehensive answers exist. Still, a lack of ready answers does not keep him from searching for a process involving values more important to the future of the American culture than arrest, threat, and punishment.

THE BIG PICTURE

There is one attribute that marks both Sullivan's and Walters's refusal to accept crime control and policing as simply a public order–maintenance agenda. This is the degree to which both men display a remarkably keen perspective on the complexity of crime and the factors that influence it, such as the town's social setting and values. Walters, as police chief, is apt to talk more about the town's economic history and growth plans than about any new programs he has designed to thwart illegal activity. In a fairly homogeneous town, Walters also demonstrates a honed sense for how intolerance and lack of involvement can come from the way city growth is managed.

In our drive around the town, Walters talks about how the town is being transformed, how a new strip mall was a dense grove of trees six years ago. He is concerned because residents in the new part of town do not see the police in the way old Mukilteo residents do. The new town folk are more isolated. Walters talks about architectural covenants that new developments create, which set color schemes for new homes, and tells me they would never go over in old town. When we talk about gated communities, he tells me about a conversation he overheard while on a bus tour during a convention in the eastern part of the state. One man asked another, "Do gated communities have any blacks?" The other man replied, "No, just Americans."

A bold and expansive view of the complex variables and social relations that go into creating crime in America is seldom explored by most politicians, let alone police chiefs. When was the last time a politician or police chief looked at a drop in crime and said, "I wish I could take credit for this, but it's probably the robust economy"? Yet that is precisely a conclusion Sullivan and Walters draw. Ensuring Mukilteo's economic vitality and trying to plan wisely for its runaway growth have become important variables in its crime-control agenda.

At one time Mukilteo served as a reserve filling station for the Pacific fleet, and to the east of the old-town waterfront sits an abandoned naval fuel tank farm. To the west is a state park, and along the waterfront sit restaurants, boutiques, and tourist-oriented shops. The old town rises southward on a steep slope along an easy-to-follow grid pattern—First Street, Second Street, Third Street. The mix of stately old Victorians and folksy, modern-shingled homes fades south of the slope as the edge of the town disappears into a tree-lined ridge.

As Chief Walters and I drive along the waterfront, he tells me that the city plans to redevelop the tank farm but that there are problems with the navy and with cleanup, and that the existing merchants are opposed to any redevelopment they feel will threaten their already precarious customer traffic. The area may become a "historic overlay zone," allowing the town to protect the land but also to redevelop it. Mukilteo's ferry run to Whidbey Island is the busiest run in Washington State. Four million tourists a year use the ferries, but they stop in Mukilteo only as long as it takes to be loaded onto one. Walters believes the city can capitalize on that traffic with redevelopment that will serve all the local merchants.

Mukilteo, like the rest of Washington State, is experiencing an economic boom. Times have been much worse; for years Mukilteo sat in the shadow of Boeing. Mayor Sullivan says the city had to face the uneasy realization that there was "a right way, a wrong way, and a Boeing way." The company owned a large parcel of land called Japanese Gulch just above the tank farm east of town. Back in the 1960s when the company was on fast expansion following the Korean War and into the Vietnam War, earthmovers operated day and night, clearing more space. Debris and felled wood were incinerated on the spot. A haze fell over Mukilteo, and the runoff from the cleared hills backed up town sewers and left a pungent sulfuric smell through the entire town. Then, in the late 1960s, the situation began to change.

In the 1970s, just as Boeing grew more concerned with how it was treating its neighbor, and as the city seized on an opportunity to annex several parcels and to regain control over what was going on, the aerospace company went bust. The whole region faced sharp layoffs. Just over the hill northeast of Mukilteo, in Everett, Boeing laid off forty thousand employees. Sullivan laughs as he recalls the local lore: "We had a saying, 'The last one to leave Seattle, turn off the lights.'" In recent years, however, the greater Seattle area has witnessed an expansive economic boom that few other regions can match. Boeing is doing better. Microsoft is soaring. Educated, skilled employees are moving into the region in droves. Completely new cities, like Federal Way, are forming to handle the growth.

Mukilteo expects more growth on top of the three hundred percent annual population increase it has experienced over the last six years. Boeing intends to expand a plant located several miles east of town. Schwinn has plans for a large bicycle factory in the town, and Seattle's need for bedrooms shows no signs of slowing. In the late afternoon, Seattle commuters retreat along the freeways and into the long, wide boulevards. They pass strip malls as they make their way to the Cape Cod– and Nantucket-style homes offering three color schemes in the new part of town. Here is where the battle to maintain community will face its biggest challenge.

Each change in the economic landscape of Mukilteo brings with it changes in the town's social structure. Old residents move out, severing ties. New residents move in, with few ties between them. The newer residents may come with little regard for town parades, a library, or other traditions and structures that represent interdependent communities. The new homes may cater to those who prefer detachment and privacy or who exhibit the trappings of new wealth, and may create what Walters observes as resentment on the part of old town residents. That is when leadership becomes crucial, not so much because of the talents and knowledge displayed by Sullivan and Walters, but because leadership can represent a certain static structure, something that remains steadfast in the face of so much change. It is from that structure that residents may find the opportunity to form those ties which will connect them with one another and will cement the bonds needed for lasting informal social control.

≈ o ≈

"We know her story," Joan Didion said in *After Henry* when she described the brutal 1989 gang rape of the New York City Central Park jogger by a band of wilding teens. When Didion told about a victim beaten so severely that fifteen months after the attack "she could not focus her eyes or walk unaided [and] she had lost all sense of smell," she intended that *her* story be *our* story. The jogger's story was a mythic narrative that spoke to us about *our* particular fears and hopes. Didion reminded us that not *all* victims' stories are our stories. The Central Park jogger was a "young woman of middle-class privilege and promise . . . New York's ideal sister, daughter, Bachrach bride." Her victimization was deeply affecting for public and politicians, though the brutal rapes of others, particularly minority women, barely receive press coverage.

Our stories are selective. The rape of a young woman with a promising career troubles us more deeply than, say, the rape of a hard-drinking trailer-park prostitute, perhaps because ours is a culture built on the notion of personal responsibility and equity: we get what we deserve, what goes around comes around, and bad karma is its own reward. Cognitive psychologists refer to this tactic for explaining people's fate as "attribution error." If we are part of the American culture, on the one hand, we tend to overattribute bad happenings faced by people we care about—or people we believe deserve better—to chance, to inescapable and tragic rare events, or to some horrible injustice. I once heard that a friend of a family member faced a rather lengthy prison term for habitual drunk driving. I suggested he might have a drinking problem. No, I was told, he was just unlucky. On the other hand, we tend to overattribute the ill fate of those we see as less deserving—those who don't play by our rules, or those from outcast groups—to their own inadequacies, laziness, personality predilections, or poor moral choices.

These are the stories all of us have heard in one form or another:

Police officers who beat suspects are aberrations, bad apples in an otherwise uncontaminated barrel. Tenacious, rule-bending detectives get the job done. Criminals are the refuse of the earth, and the only way to respond to them is to burn them out of their homes or lock them away forever. Controlling crime means maintaining order by clamping on law violations.

The story of Sullivan and Walters comes early in a book about community power for a reason. A glimpse at their leadership styles reminds us that even in stories about problem solving that is indigenous to communities, even in the world of citizen power, leaders are people who can and must play an important role. Leaders are part of a community. Moreover, Sullivan's and Walters's stories should encourage us because people such as politicians and police chiefs, people who potentially have the most reason to cling to their conceptual security blankets, can embrace other perspectives.

Their story can become our own. Their story must become our own because we cannot rely solely on leaders to achieve what must come from our own ambitions. Indeed, in Mukilteo's case, Walters will move on to bigger challenges and Sullivan will not seek another term, at least, for the time being, thus avoiding more direct hits from snowballs and castigations at parades. Leaders can provide the help to develop and maintain a structure, but it is up to us to seek public servants who share a vision for community. They must make us aware that even if what we currently do to reduce crime seems efficacious in terms of lowering those oft-quoted statistics, we must not rest. Sullivan and Walters remind us never to shy away from asking whether the things that we do really address the needs that crime represents, whether the things that we do really mark the best of what a democratic culture such as our own should demand of itself.

Sullivan and Walters are not afraid of a model that sees crime control as dependent not on *Starsky and Hutch*–like freewheeling detectives but on an unglamorous group of citizens casually gathered on a neighbor's lawn some warm spring evening, and on benevolent city officials willing to grasp the big picture, no matter how complex. Sullivan and Walters would rather their town devise an eloquent redevelopment plan than a sophisticated, computerized crime-mapping program, and they would rather develop social relations that might encourage informal social control than throw people in jail. Their role requires boldness and honesty. Even within an apparently idyllic and most promising city, Sullivan and Walters are bold enough to expose the problems, to wrestle with them, and to demand something more. Their roles require complete openness and a desire for participation from all members of the community. Theirs are stories that we should get to know and make our own.

2. No Humans Involved

Policing with community in mind

To get the good stuff, you gotta be on foot.
—Police officer on the television show *COPS*

The "good stuff" for the real-life officer on the popular real-life television show *COPS*, quoted in the epigraph, was, in police parlance, a "righteous bust." He effected such a bust while on foot patrol, and his words indicate an ability to use foot patrol stealthily to observe a suspected drug dealer and then to swoop in for a tidy seizure of drugs and a career-enhancing arrest. He realized that the insular environment of the patrol car does not afford officers intimate contact with the offenses potentially taking place on their beats. He also voiced a common perception about the power afforded officers who police using a style called "community policing." It is a return to a nostalgic image of patrol officers walking a beat. In focusing on arrest, the officer signaled what community policing has become for many cities: a way to increase the state intervention apparatus through arrest by using the community to help identify, locate, and detail illegal activity.

Officers strolling the sidewalks in our neighborhoods might evoke romantic images such as a patrolman stopping to assist a child with a broken bike, helping a resident pull-start a gas lawn mower, or checking to make sure nothing appears unusual in the neighborhood. In its most narrow conception, community policing is supposed to evoke those images. It is supposed to involve officers with the community, involve the community with officers, and involve all

34

in a quest to make neighborhoods safer. Unfortunately, though, however unintentionally, the movement to embrace community-policing practices creates limited roles for both officers and community members. These roles negate latent problem-solving skills indigenous to the community—skills that might help treat or reduce deviant behavior—in favor of the community's becoming a booster for officers. The officers' cultural climate remains inhospitable toward a community's informal problem-solving abilities, favoring instead an officer's intervention repertoire and worldview on crime control. The net effect is a crime-control model that disturbs community ecology more than stabilizes it, one in which officers fail to fully exploit cohesive, resourceful community networks, in favor of surveillance, crackdowns, sweeps, arrests, and problem obliteration.

THE QUEST

On Interstate 90 in eastern Washington State, a quintessential old railroad town appears out of the semiarid scrub and grasslands stretching to Idaho. This is Spokane, a place small enough and obscure enough that a typical cross-country traveler probably would not go beyond stopping for a tank of gas or a quick bite to eat. The traveler who does explore it further will discover a world undergoing transformation. As if it were a practiced slogan, town residents I met invariably mentioned that Spokane is the most populous city on the northern latitude between Seattle and Chicago. They are proud that the city of some three hundred thousand has experienced unexpected growth in the last decade, growth that has nearly doubled home values in some neighborhoods.

Spokane has all the offerings of Seattle—concerts, fairs, parks, plays, a symphony, and a prestigious annual footrace. But an unmistakable competition, marked by an inferiority complex, exists between Spokane and its sophisticated cultural powerhouse to the west. I had come to expect constant comparisons with life elsewhere on the West Coast, because nearly everyone in Spokane is a transplant from some more sophisticated big city. Changes taking place in Spokane are important to understand, because it is a modern city sown from the seeds of discontentment and fear. The lure for its new arrivals is that it offers a big-city feel with small-town security, a nostalgic idea of the past. Newcomers see Spokane as a city safe from all those urban problems that have seeped into other once-desirable sites such as Portland and Seattle.

The Pacific Northwest as a whole is a story about transient people searching for a past that may never have existed. Many residents I met talked about Idaho, particularly Boise, with admiration. When those urban problems that are always nipping at their heels become too great for them in Spokane, perhaps they will move on to Boise. One family enjoyed a middle-class existence, but during the last twelve years its members had made a wandering journey in search of that better life. Before Spokane they had lived in Seattle. Before Seattle, Portland. Before Portland, the San Francisco Bay area. Before that, Los Angeles. Before Los Angeles, it was the Midwest.

If not the Midwest, it is the Northeast, or sometimes the South, that serves as the original site in these stories about a vanguard toward El Dorado. Each starting point remains a long-ago memory; each past stopping point becomes a painful abortion. Still, these Spokane families believe the Grail awaits them, and the search for it consumes their discussions around the dinner table, afternoon visits with friends, and interviews with researchers from one of those rat-race cities they fled.

They left their little towns in those faraway places riding a wave of prosperity on the West Coast, one that promised high-paying jobs and the resulting good life. What they found failed to satiate them, and the longing developed into a nostalgic search for a simpler life and an elusive community. Problems such as crime ruined the fantasy, and now they undertake one move after another. As one community activist in Spokane told me, "I did the whole rat-race thing. I thought quality of life was living in a waterside condo, working ninety hours a week to make it work. I was going crazy." She lamented that she had enrolled her son in day care at three months so she could make the lifestyle work and that now, as a teenager, her son wants nothing to do with school. With a tired eloquence she said she bought into the cultural paradigm of the *Better Homes and Gardens* house, the fancy car, and the expensive amenities, only to decide that it was not the only option, that something more social might be better. "I knew," she said as her voice trailed off, "there was something more." Others like her who decided that Spokane would mark the end of their journey decided to make a stand. In this modern American saga, community policing would serve as the marshal riding into town to save their ideal existence from an uncertain and scary future marked by crime, poverty, and urban decay.

COP BOOSTERS

Spokane's northeast Hillyard neighborhood was built around a turn-of-the-century railroad yard, the largest in the United States. The neighborhood was marked first by the rowdy, brawling atmosphere of stockyards and the railroad, later by the decline of the railroad in American life, and finally by the increase in the problems associated with urban decay. Today in an association formed to fight crime and improve the neighborhood, twenty-nine active members base themselves in a burned-out tavern. Hillyard is now a neighborhood strewn with the skeletons of taverns past and the wretched facades of taverns present.

The pride of the Hillyard Association is its Friday Night Gym. Every week as many as three hundred youths take part in volleyball or basketball games, receive informal coaching for a variety of sports activities, and learn more about police department youth activities such as STARS (Smart Teens Are Responsible and Sober), LEAD (the Leadership, Education, and Development Program), COPY Kids (Community Opportunities Program for Youth), and DARE (Drug Abuse Resistance Education).

The small but eager group of Hillyard volunteers say that the best part of these Friday night sessions is the attendance of their Neighborhood Resource Officer (NRO). The NRO is Spokane's version of the officer on the beat, an individual tied into the community's pulse. Departmental marketing material describes the NRO "as part of the Spokane Police Department's commitment to a community empowerment model of policing." The NRO typically works on problems ranging from neighborhood disputes and nuisance abatement to drug and gang activity. Another departmental guide advises, "The officers often work directly with families whose children have been identified as 'at risk' by school staff members. . . .

They are invited into classrooms to talk with students about self-esteem, drugs, alcohol abuse, gangs and abuse."

When it comes to community efforts to reduce crime, Hillyard Association members reserve nearly all their praise for their NRO. Many volunteers come from the retired ranks of the Anglo community. The Spokane Police Department vigorously recruits from this pool, encouraging retired residents to serve as community service personnel, citizen patrol members, and neighborhood liaisons. Programs like the Friday night sessions have brought elderly members of the community together with young members and bridged a chasm once filled with misunderstanding, fear, and stereotypes. The volunteers say that they are surprised to have come to see the youths in a different light—a positive light—and they find the experience encouraging. Although some youths who attend the Friday night events share a similar surprise at finding older volunteers helping on projects and at enjoying the rapport developing between the two groups, the NRO's presence remains the focus. One NRO, responding to the heightened demands put on him as community problem solver, printed a "message from your NRO" in large bold letters in the association newsletter to remind the volunteers: "I have mentioned it time and time again: Please take most calls when I am here as if I wasn't here. I am always working on previous calls or other duties when I am here."

Like residents in other cities I visited, Spokane citizens downplayed their own roles in the process of establishing relations across disparate groups. They focused both on their NROs or their versions of community police officers and on the general law enforcement function. In Portland, Oregon, one neighborhood coalition member beamed when she recounted that cops had driven around the neighborhood telling youths during a particularly hot spell that the local pools were open. In the preceding twenty years, relations with the police had fallen to such a low that now any positive, nonauthoritarian contact receives similar exaltation.

The Spokane Police Department remains a national leader in developing programs designed to change the public's perceptions of officers, develop dialogue with youths, and acquaint citizens, as a department flyer states, "with law enforcement's role in serving and protecting the community." One glossy and colorful department report says the department offers twenty-eight core programs. These include the teen-oriented programs listed earlier, as well as the following: Cops & Kids, an annual police-sponsored professional car show and SWAT and K-9 unit demonstration; Trading Cards, the production of collectible cards depicting patrol officers; Knock & Nag, "a program to educate the public on security issues and on the importance of Operation Identification" (which marks valuables with owners' driver's license numbers); and Block Braggers, an effort that has provided litter bags to neighborhood residents, and charts residents' "bragging" about "a new job, kids doing well in school, home improvements, etc. . . . . A block leader then charts block improvements on an area map. . . . At the end of the year, the block with the most improvements receives a block party."

One consequence of these programs is that in some cases the beat officers develop very close bonds with the residents they serve. For their part, the residents become boosters for the officers. The Hillyard neighborhood's NRO wanted to advance in the department, and advancement meant leaving his place in their neighborhood. The residents felt a profound loss, but the loss also gave the group impetus for finding a suitable replacement, an action that was acceptable to the police chief. As one resident told me, "We knew his wife, his whole family. It was a very sad loss, and it was hard to lose such an influential person in our community. When the replacement was considered, we interviewed the five who applied and sent the chief our recommendations for who we wanted." Another local volunteer in a different Spokane neighborhood saw his job as making the beat officer comfortable by bringing him snacks and treats and ensuring that the officer had quiet time when he filled out reports in the neighborhood substation.

Three years ago in Hillyard, 40 percent of the storefronts were vacant, the neighborhood had the largest number of rental vacancies in the city, and, according to residents, most of the cars driving through the neighborhood were filled with drug buyers or drug dealers. All that has changed for the better, and the citizens involved in the community-policing project feel optimistic. The dependency of the community, however, on the community-policing officer creates potential complications, especially when the department's and the officers' working orientation differs from the community's. The culture of the police department remains hamstrung by stereotypes and a siege mentality from the chief on down to the rank-and-file officers.

A CULTURE HOSTILE TO COMMUNITY

During my stay in Spokane, the police chief was the subject of a news story detailing how he pulled a gun on the occupants of a car parked near his driveway. They were playing a CB-radio version of hide-and-seek and were waiting for further instructions when the chief went to investigate. After some heated questioning by the chief, the occupants were allowed to leave. On a previous occasion the chief was involved in a traffic collision after he pursued youths who flipped him off while passing in a car. Some minority residents told me that on another occasion the chief's temper flared at a community meeting called to reconcile grievances about police and citizen patrols in one neighborhood.

In the administrative ranks of the department, Assistant Chief David Ingle is willing to analyze the apparent paradox posed by a chief who takes an aggressive attitude while trying to govern a department that provides the public with brochures stating "a year 2000 goal to . . . be a culturally diverse, highly motivated, professional law enforcement organization representative of and respected by the community it serves." Ingle, a part-time college instructor, laments the difficulty of making what he calls institutional change. Ingle teaches courses in management and community-policing principles and peppers his analysis with statements about the phases of transformational change and the necessary steps to institutional change.

Toward the end of the interview, after refilling his coffee, he relaxes some and leans back in his chair. He then tells me a story that defines the department's culture more powerfully than any multi-point plan for change, vision statement, or glossy guide to programs I have yet read. He tells me about a drive-by shooting in one of the lower-income neighborhoods. The assailants killed two young girls, both innocent bystanders. Ingle's recollection is that the officers on the scene felt little distress about the situation, noting that it was just another NHI shooting. (NHI is a police abbreviation for the phrase "No Humans Involved.") Ingle's story is not a justification for the officers' heartless feelings but an illustration of the way police work creates severe impediments to caring about people, which is precisely what community policing, when practiced to its fullest, requires of an officer.

A Spokane departmental training handbook contains an essay by a professor from a college in the Southeast explaining that he became a police officer to experience firsthand the world an officer patrols. The professor confesses that he once spoke out strongly against excessive use of police force but that after a few days on the job he wanted to do a little head bashing himself. His revelation is hardly a new insight. Such views are well documented in criminological literature: graduate students who are sent to observe the police at work soon condone actions they previously would have abhorred; researchers get caught up in off-duty activities with officers and blur the line between objectivity and involvement.

We assume this effect stems from the cultural climate of policing, that seeing the worst of human behavior day after day makes officers toss much of their compassion aside. But perhaps the answer rests with something a little different and more troubling. The police are given a tremendous amount of authority. As Harrison Ford's character Rick Deckard is told in the movie *Bladerunner,* "If you're not cop, you're little people!" With that intoxicating authority the police are expected to solve a wide array of problems. Time and time again I witnessed citizen groups deferring their indigenous abilities to the trained professional. Because paramilitary organizations relying on arrest will most likely never resolve social ills, the officer is set up for a fall, frustration ensues, and a reaction is not far behind.

As a group, police officers suffer from disturbing rates of spousal abuse, alcoholism, and suicide. Police hold the mace of authority, the power of life or death, over the rest of us. If association with this power can intoxicate even the most objective researchers and those close to policing, it is no wonder that officers see the application of authority as the answer to problems. When problems refuse to subside, the concentration and application of more power and authority becomes the solution. Paradoxically, a democracy thrives on the distribution of power; hence, the police come from a microculture quite at odds with the macroculture in which they function.

"Everybody likes firemen," one citizen volunteer told me in Mukilteo, Washington, "but not everyone likes police. We've got to get the community behind the police as much as they are behind the firemen." Despite the glaring differences between police officers and firefighters, this volunteer's words make me wonder whether community policing ultimately serves to make the police feel better about their mission and the community more supportive of that mission, and whether debating needed cultural shifts in policing is an unnecessary theoretical abstraction.

A week later I am in Oregon City, Oregon, where a police recruit on the job for less than three weeks talks to me about this distressing paradox faced by police. He explains that he spent a great deal of time training in community policing. His field training manual was full of terms like *empowerment* and *collaboration,* but it also observed that community policing was "in addition to, and not a substitute for traditional law enforcement duties." "Once an arrest has been made," another passage from the manual advised, "and the guilty party has been packed off to jail, the officer must ask himself/herself, 'Does this solve the problem? Or is it just another arrest in a long line of arrests for the same crime in the same place?'"

The recruit tells about a complaint he and his field training officer (FTO) responded to. A resident's dog was frequently seen urinating on a neighbor's lawn. The "victim" wanted his neighbor cited. The young recruit suggested that the "victim" talk to her neighbor, but the "victim" did not want anything to do with it. "She refused and just kept saying, 'You handle it,'" the recruit observes. "Now the manual says to try creative stuff, but what am I going to tell her besides talk to her neighbor? Besides, my FTO wouldn't look kindly on some other strategy, so I just produced a citation. I know that it would probably just increase animosity between the neighbors, but what else could I do?"

As community-based responses fail to surface, the police resort to the tried-and-true process whereby they receive complaints and use citizens to assist in the law enforcement enterprise. This process has become so standard that it is now seen as the normal community-policing strategy. As a special neighborhood liaison in Portland put it, "Community policing is really about better communication with police and citizens seeing responsibility for resolving the problem on both sides. The citizen says, 'Why can't you just do it?' So the officer talks about a process: 'You have to work together to provide me with information and be willing to back me up in a court of law.'" The officer does not want to disappoint his or her staunchest supporters—the community—but the officer's tools to win their favor do not offer any radical departure from the traditional law enforcement mission.

When it comes to actual law enforcement duties, all parties involved with the community-policing project express a clear understanding of their limited role. Still, despite the warning one volunteer gave, "You get into trouble if an NRO is expected to be the power, and there's a fine line that an officer doesn't cross except by request," the reality is that the community officer carries a great deal of prestige and influence, and shapes the direction taken by community crime fighting. If getting the good stuff means increasing arrests for the officer and in turn aiding in his or her advancement, then the community will assist in gaining those goods.

A study of patrol time usage in the Houston, Texas, police department revealed that most line officers did not believe attending neighborhood meetings was "real police work" and, worse still, erroneously believed they had very little free time to pursue community-based practices. The officers' view of time was skewed by their tendency to "wolf-pack," or show up en masse on calls because that was where the excitement—the good stuff—was. In regard to Santa Ana, California, getting the good stuff creates the potential for a socio-ecological disaster in the city.

A NEIGHBORHOOD'S GOOD STUFF

At first glance Santa Ana is an altogether different city from Spokane. A dense, urban environment nestled between predominantly Anglo Orange County suburbs and affluent beach communities, the city has entrenched gangs, no shortage of drug dealing, and a steady array of crimes. At the same time, its burgeoning Latino population, like its middle-class, mostly Anglo Pacific Northwest counterpart, is searching for a better life.

Like Spokane, Santa Ana has a nationally recognized police department that adheres to a community-policing model that the department has successfully marketed. Santa Ana also provides a case study of the inherent dilemma posed by current community policing. Its department produces innovative and aggressive community-based policing strategies, but it has failed to identify and exploit fully any latent problem-solving abilities indigenous to the neighborhoods.

Santa Ana has developed several programs all under the community-policing rubric: Operation Weed and Seed, Operation Round-Up, the Street Terrorist Offender Project, and the COP Task Force. All of the programs depend in large measure on arrest as the main problem-solving tool. Santa Ana relies heavily on the model that Chief Walters in chapter 1 bemoaned, the one that requires officers to arrest or threaten arrest for even the most minor violations. Santa Ana's chief, Paul Walters, explained his policies to the *Orange County Register:* "You've still got to arrest people. You've still got to hold them and deal with prosecutors. But that's not the end. You don't have change. You've got to do more."

Doing more was the initial concept behind Operation Weed and Seed, a policing strategy spearheaded and disseminated by federally funded programs during the Bush administration. "Weed and seed" meant that police would raid a neighborhood as a follow-up to investigative work that had developed cases against suspected criminals there. The police arrested the criminals, joint task forces of federal, state, and local prosecutors would throw the book at them, and that would be that. Recognizing that future criminals might simply spring up—like weeds—in the void left by the previous criminals, the model then called for police and other agencies to move in with preventive programs—"seeds"—to keep criminal activity from coming back.

As part of Weed and Seed, Santa Ana pushes to redevelop slum property, and offers educational programs and job skills training. Problems with Weed and Seed strategies arise because crime is a complex phenomenon, dependent on a complex web of networks and relations that do not always fit the neat geographic locations used to define a community.

Today I am in Santa Ana. Although Santa Ana reports that its residents feel safer and crime has dropped, a community activist I meet is troubled by the message delivered in Santa Ana's community-policing process. He points to Operation Round-Up as an example.

Operation Round-Up is the pride of Santa Ana's nationally recognized model for how a department and community can come together to solve a major crime epidemic. For several months in 1994, police, prosecutors, and a special federal task force compiled evidence against one of the worst gangs in the city. In a massive one-night sweep, the task force rounded up thirteen suspected gang members and arrested them on a variety of charges. Santa Ana lieutenant Bill Tegler, who shows slide programs to audiences across the country chronicling the success of Round-Up, takes pride in telling his listeners that, thanks to the gang members' previous records and the extensive investigative work, the suspects were eligible for three-strikes prosecution, meaning the teen terrorists all faced sentences of twenty-five years to life in California prisons.

The troubling part for the community activist I meet is that, although there is no disputing that the kids were no saints, any policy grounded on arrest was problematic, because in one fell swoop the police showed how easy it was to wipe out a sizable part of the young lifeblood in that neighborhood. This is not to say the gang members made a positive contribution in their neighborhood. The activist contends that the point is not to excuse the gangs' actions or to underestimate the terror they spread, but to understand the complexity of the problem and the fact that the gang members could have represented a positive youth force in the community if some preventive effort had been made earlier. That potential is now lost.

I think back to Trojanowicz's notion of community policing exemplified by the teens in a vandalized park who were given some responsibility for the park's upkeep. The good stuff for policing is still the grand bust, the major crackdown, the adrenaline-inducing chase. Where is the romance in requesting that bothersome teens take a place at the community table? Where is the immediate reward, the excitement, in trying to tackle a complicated problem down a long and wearisome path?

The ease with which the community-policing model operates, the activist reasons, shows the police in a positive light and wins the backing of some local residents, but that is not what all the residents want or what can bring long-term change to the neighborhoods. There is a central dilemma for policing, illustrated by the community-policing stories in this chapter. Despite much ballyhoo about community policing being more proactive, the policing culture tends toward a stranded position of reactive crime fighting and short-term rewards. The activist outlines the dilemma thus: "Suppose the new seed programs don't take; then the process will just repeat. The chief says he polices based on a policy of community wellness, but all he's doing well is wiping out the youth of our community."

≈ o ≈

I have Santa Ana on my mind when I visit Portland, where I discuss some of the troubling prospects raised by Weed and Seed with another community activist. She responds with a story resembling a parable: During a neighborhood meeting to discuss closing down a hotel known for prostitution and drug sales, one woman stood up, nervously identified herself as a resident of the hotel, and then said she was one of those dope users. She was one of the problems, and she had come to the community meeting because she wanted to be a part of the community. Others wanted to condemn the hotel, but that meant condemning her. She agreed that they should do something, and then broke down in tears, crying, "But I don't want to be on the needle; what about me?" Some in attendance showed sympathy. Others were unmoved. But all reflected on the lack of alternative ways to address the problem the hotel presented in the neighborhood.

The community-policed world allows little room for error or time to stop and think about justice. Rather, it attempts to make justice work more smoothly, to enjoin communities in a speedy and effective process. If the outcome that policy makers aim for is a sense of safety and security, then perhaps the model succeeds. If, on the other hand, the outcome sought looks like the world that Chief Walters and Mayor Sullivan envision, then there is much room to improve. Where can that dope user go to receive help to overcome her habit when the community is engaged in a war against her? Where can a sex offender go to ask for assistance to keep from offending when the community wants to burn him out of his home? Where can a drug dealer go to find a legitimate trade when he is a pariah?

Community policing has yet to become a way to find people who may be predisposed to crime and to help them beat the odds. Currently, it is a way to find people who may be predisposed to crime in order to remove them from the community or to increase control over them. Because the problem-solving repertoire of the police depends heavily on arrest, community members who otherwise might come forward as potential offenders in order to seek preventive community support remain silent. Community policing has yet to provide room for open discussion of problems and admission of wrongdoing. The community itself, however, need not approach a problem with a similar framework, because communities are not bound by law to arrest offenders.

In defining the roles police and community members can play in the process, Hank Elliott, a community volunteer in Mukilteo, Washington, said, "It's important to cultivate relationships whether they're based on the job, family, or your own recreational pursuits." Elliott, a retired military officer, explained that he never appreciated the value of finding community among his neighbors and friends, because he was always moving from one assignment to the next. When he finally retired, he said that he "really started to understand the need to get to know each other. The goal is not to accentuate our differences and find ways to single people out for arrest or whatever, but to find communality among our differences, to build something based on that. You don't want to piss someone off you care about."

A self-proclaimed Portland "old-timer" said that infatuation with crime and building community was just part of a cycle, that every twenty years or so a new crop of young people move in, want to have families, and want to change things. She wondered why no effort is made to have each generation feed off the energy of the next so that the process of change never ends. The only stumbling block to efforts proposed by Elliott, the old-timer, and others is the police—the very entity saddled with the burden to produce those results in contemporary neighborhoods everywhere.

The saga continues to play out in cities across the United States and around the world. Community policing, without a doubt, has become the ubiquitous model for policing. When, how, and where community policing finally succeeds will depend on what the stories reveal. In places such as Spokane, the story represents a quest for a quality of life previously jeopardized by crime and a dizzying urban pace. This is a story most of us know all too well.

Community policing is embraced as a deliverer from the worries of crime, but in that embrace there is less effort toward "collective efficacy," toward recognizing the roles citizens might take irrespective of the police, roles that only the citizens can perform. In that embrace there is little regard for much-needed cultural transformation in policing. In places such as Mukilteo, Oregon City, and Portland, the story represents an overappreciation for the ability police have to solve problems and an underappreciation for a connected community's power to find solutions. In places such as Santa Ana, preventing and responding to crime always involves human actors who possess human imperfections and the complications of messy, flawed lives.

The stories we do not know well enough may be the ones that help us form connections across our communities; allow us to develop our own problem-solving skills, which the police can assist but cannot define or direct; encourage us to allow those on the edge of the community to come forward and to draw on the community's strength in order to stay clear of crime; and make us realize that control could just as well come from creating stable and resource-rich local ecologies rather than seeking retribution-minded justice. In the next chapter we find such a story. As in previous stories, problems exist, but the awareness of hurdles need not cause dismay. Indeed, crime control through community building may mean no more than redefining what it means for police to "get the good stuff" when humans are involved.

3. Spy Shops and Nasty Old People

Residents mobilizing with cops to build community

This is as close as I'll ever get to being a cop.
—Neighborhood coalition leader in Portland,
Oregon

During the 1980s, Portland's southeast neighborhoods were undergoing a transition from their predominately white, working-class base to include a demographic blend of young gays, Asian Americans, and Latinos. Even though Oregon's economy lagged during the 1970s and into the early 1980s, a steady stream of young, professional, white-collar transplants from California and other states migrated to the region in search of lower housing costs and a more tranquil quality of life. Homes cost less, so home buyers received a lot more for their money. Absent from Portland neighborhoods were mass-produced, monotonous tract homes. Instead buyers found an appealing selection, from turn-of-the-century fixer-upper Victorians to post–World War II stucco ranch homes.

After the new residents moved in, the market reflected both the improvements made to the properties and the demand for Portland homes. The once relatively inexpensive homes historically owned by the working-class residents of these neighborhoods, some of whom had lived under the same roof for three generations, soon were assessed property taxes far above what they could afford. All around Portland and its suburbs the story was repeated. Lake Oswego, some ten miles to the south, became a bedroom community for the well-to-do. There, huge, multistory stone mansions began to spring up alongside decaying single-story clapboard bungalows. When a long-time resident's home was finally put on the market, a buyer or developer snatched it up only to level the property and build a mansion on the land.

The uncertain economic and social futures of the working class provided the opportunity for someone like Tom Metzger and his White Aryan Resistance (WAR) group to foment hatred and scape-goating. The southeast neighborhoods became the base of large and active skinhead groups, recruited mostly from the working-class families that once had dominated the neighborhood. Vandalism, spray-painted swastikas, and derogatory slogans scribbled on businesses and homes became commonplace.

On a fall night in 1988, following an evening of drinking, three skinheads from a group calling itself Eastside Pride stumbled upon Mulugeta Seraw, an Ethiopian exchange student. In the ensuing attack, one of the three took a full swing with a baseball bat to the back of Seraw's head. As Seraw fell to the pavement, the group kicked his body with their steel-toed boots. The three were eventually prosecuted for Seraw's murder.

The task of restoring some understanding across race and class lines in the southeast neighborhoods and of reducing the vitriolic rhetoric of organizations like WAR fell upon Katherine Anderson and the Southeast Uplift, a program for which she is the crime prevention specialist.

Portland has a history of active and effective neighborhood coalitions spread across the city. Coalitions like Southeast Uplift were formed in the late 1960s primarily to address land-use issues. They also mounted a grassroots campaign to improve the quality of life for inner-Portland residents, and gave a voice to neighborhood demands for improved community development. In some cases the coalitions remain dynamic, providing an eclectic array of services that seek to locate and resolve problems by empowering and exploiting indigenous community power. In all cases, however, the coalitions have taken center stage in a new war, the war on crime. In an emerging trend, citizen groups such as these are being teamed with police or other official government entities.

Anderson's office, a hot room without air-conditioning in an old brick church that has housed a number of civic programs, reveals the influence this new war has had on the agency's activities. This room is decorated in contemporary crime-prevention chic: walls lined with posters for National Night Out against Crime, literature for drug prevention and DARE programs, and neighborhood newsletters. Stickers, key chains, and other crime-prevention paraphernalia are scattered, stacked, and boxed around the office. As I survey this scene, my expression must give something away, because Anderson quickly tells me, "We do a lot of other things, more than just crime prevention."

As we move outside to sit under a cool arbor, Anderson points to the neighborhood around her and relates how the coalition handled the area's hate groups, a problem that she is confident has been reduced. Anderson believes the key for the coalition is to make area residents realize that neither harassment nor arrest offers constructive reactions. For example, in dealing with the skinhead activity, she emphasized, the key was to invite all the parties to the table and to work toward a central value shift in their thinking. It was no easy task to convince alienated youth to attend a discussion on cultural understanding and tolerance, but with some cajoling by the police and other neighborhood influences, a process was started that led to a successful series of meetings that in turn seemed to reduce attacks in the area. Anderson concedes that skinhead activity also slowed following Tom Metzger's trial for conspiracy in Seraw's death.

The process begun by the coalition required discussion participants to refrain from name-calling and accusations, but everything else was permissible. Involved residents from various class and race segments in the neighborhoods were encouraged to discuss grievances and to talk together to reach a common understanding. Anderson says everyone in the neighborhood tried to take roles of one type or another and expressed unique viewpoints, even the skinheads. Residents began to see their integral links to one another: businesses needed to keep liquor licenses, so their owners needed to appreciate and respect their neighbors; youths wanted autonomy, so they needed to know what behaviors would lead to city intervention and what it would take for neighbors to leave them alone. "It was really a series on good neighboring," says Anderson. "We have these citizen police academies, but what about good-neighboring academies? How many times do we see our neighbors over positive things versus negative things? Community and youth programs also always seem so separate. They should all be united in the process."

Anderson notes that an important goal for the coalition was not only to sponsor the diversity meetings but also to increase area celebration, with events such as multicultural festivals. "Organizing for events in the neighborhood is one good way to bring people together . . . because it requires so many different entities communicating and working together."

As Anderson sees it, the successful prevention of and response to hate crimes in southeast Portland neighborhoods was not a job for the police. They attempt to remove offenders from given sites but do nothing to shape the culture that may have encouraged the offenses. "Bias crime is not something addressed by police departments very effectively," she notes, adding, "nor are issues like drugs and prostitution. These are life-coping-skills problems created by the person's living environment." And who is better placed to address those skills, the police or an offender's friends and neighbors? Like the activist in Santa Ana, Anderson is uneasy with the increasing law enforcement response to hate and bias crime, because such a response tends to take aim at individual actors rather than the entire social environment an actor inhabits. At the same time, however, Anderson works closely with the police.

In view of the apparent change in mission of Southeast Neighborhood Uplift, from that of social activism aimed toward general community improvement to that of a quasipolice function, I ask Anderson whether this creates a paradox or reflects a trend away from citizen-based problem solving to an uneasy, scripted relationship with the police. She notes that the police are receiving unprecedented financial resources and political support, so it makes sense to direct some of those resources toward community ventures.

I am still left with the question, Is the community reshaping the police mission or are the police co-opting community resources for their own agenda? The evidence points to the Portland Police Bureau's increasing dependence on the neighborhood coalitions in a process that may make the coalitions a quasipolice arm rather than making the police another responsive city service available to neighborhoods engaged in grassroots problem solving. Generally, the relationship between police and coalitions first involves the police calling a coalition with information about a problem brought to the police bureau's attention; or the coalition may call the police regarding some ongoing problem. Next, the sergeant who serves as a liaison with the coalition will instruct coalition crime-prevention specialists or crime-prevention program managers on various remedies provided by law. The coalition may request more information about the problem, and then mobilizes residents to respond. For example, gang activity involving Asian Americans at a middle school resulted in a series of meetings between Asian Americans and the police bureau. Driving home the reality of gangs to some parents was the major hurdle, and the remaining response required education sessions about how parents could involve themselves with their children's activities to prevent their kids from getting into trouble. "The key," Anderson advises, "is developing an action plan and then be willing to take action, whether it be calling the police, reporting crime, documenting it, talking to neighbors about activity, [or] supporting neighbors against retaliation."

One state away, in Spokane, and in Santa Ana, retaliation is also a principal theme. In a high-crime neighborhood in Spokane, the Neighborhood Resource Officer explains that apathy is not the biggest problem with which area organizers must contend. The NRO seems to think that residents in high-crime areas fear retaliation and that this fear blocks many potentially beneficial citizen anticrime movements. As I investigated the complex social environment and role structure in which a retaliatory atmosphere develops, two major difficulties were revealed. First, the current policing structure is oriented such that the power afforded police and their allies must invariably take aim at a human target—a human transgressor, someone they can arrest—rather than a social system. This can increase tension in neighborhoods and weaken cohesive bonds between residents. Second, police-led interventions, by design, steer clear of political action and try to maintain a naive, apolitical state in areas highly charged with political tension. In the next section I will diagram how this results in a lack of motivation toward crime-reduction programs or narrowly directs capable and willing community power toward police-engineered programmatic inventions.

SPY SHOPS AND RETALIATION

The geographic tracking of crime is currently de rigueur among academicians and police agencies. Problem-oriented policing, as discussed in the introduction, requires departments to track problem locations or areas where repeated calls for service burden police resources. Police departments have found a tactical advantage in using computer-generated mapping, marking calls for service on large city maps—much like those shown in war-room scenes in movies—and then targeting certain hot spots for crackdowns.

The mapping strategy generates its own geographic dimensions that sometimes cross patrol sectors, which themselves are often determined by random and outdated department practices. In this flux, community policing seeks to rely on community groups that typically define their operations on an entirely different set of variables, such as the location of a few key leaders or an existing and efficient resource network. Also, multiple leaders may organize different groups in the same location, because each group's leader may hold a different perception about what type of intervention is required. As a result, community anticrime efforts based on geographic data or patrol-beat locations will neglect social relations that cross geographic boundaries (I will discuss more of these "social network" implications in chapter 6).

For example, consider the fairly straightforward traffic problem in Mukilteo as cars flew over the crest of a street on the edge of town. A simple compilation of statistical reports might have highlighted that particular location as the site of frequent accidents. Chief Walters might have devised and implemented some strategy to increase traffic safety at the spot without ever involving the community directly. He knew, however, that involving the community in that one problem would forge relationships and alliances. He might need to rely on those relationships in more complex situations in the future; and, as it turned out, the solution to the traffic problem was far from straightforward.

Now consider an infinitely more complex problem: the gang

activity in Santa Ana. The complexity of this problem arises because its causes, consequences, and solution no doubt encompass issues ranging across geographic boundaries that are intertwined with various social relations. To a large extent, crime mapping neglects those social relations.

Suppose each gang incident becomes a color-coded icon on a crime map. Suppose the activity of each gang member is tracked through field contact cards filled out by police officers each time they happen across a known gang member, and each of these contacts is also given a dot on the crime map. From a tactical standpoint, this information is useful for the police in aiding deployment of resources and developing response procedures.

However, this approach also carries some costs. For one, it is much easier to make war on a group of subjects when they become abstract representations on a map. Additionally, because an understanding of complex social relations is absent in the graphic representation of single events, it is too easy to focus on those incidents, a habit which, in turn, may lead to an eradication or crackdown mentality. For the time being, crime (as represented by the data) may subside, but as the activist in Santa Ana tried to articulate, and as biologists have known for decades, eradicating a weed without fully comprehending the ecological balance of the ecosystem in which the plant exists may further disrupt, rather than stabilize, that system. Why should human ecological arrangements be any less interrelated than plant and other animal systems? In human terms, symptoms of disruption may start with alienation or a sense of acquiescence to the problem-solving repertoire of the police, and eventually may reduce social ties the existence of which can prove more helpful in long-term social control than all the high-tech computer maps money can buy.

Perhaps the most harmful consequence of this focus on geography is that socially defined citizen responses suffer from a lack of structural support and resources provided by the city, because such resources likely come in a form defined by geographic borders. Such is the case with neighborhood-based police substations, or COP Shops, as they are called in Spokane. COPS West was the first substation established in Spokane, instituted by Cheryl Steele, a Seattle area transplant–turned–community activist. Once an indignant resident who mobilized neighbors in response to a brutal crime in her neighborhood—the abduction of two local girls—one of whom was later found murdered, Steele now holds a paying job with Spokane as the program coordinator for community-oriented policing services. On the day I visit I see tokens of national recognition for Steele lining the COPS West station walls: a picture of Steele with President Clinton, several citations, and news stories about how she became involved in community anticrime efforts. The common theme I found while interviewing individuals involved in neighborhood response was that, although they themselves had not always been the victim, they had experienced crime very closely and felt a need to do something about it.

Steele left the West Coast rat race and a mortgage of a thousand dollars a month for a simpler lifestyle and a three-hundred-dollar monthly mortgage in Spokane. She was so intoxicated by Spokane's spirit, a nostalgic sidewalk-strolling, get-to-know-your-neighbor feel, that she realized that even if Spokane lacked the employment resources found in the rich, high-tech coast cities, living in the area required much less earning power. As Steele puts it, "Hell, I'd flip burgers at the local burger joint if that's the only kind of job I'd get."

Steele is forward and outspoken. I am surprised by her appearance, expecting perhaps an overworked, out-of-shape, chain-smoking public activist or a beehive-hairdoed, tight-collared, conservative anticrime reactionary. Instead I meet a woman youthful in attire and presence—most notably sporting a fashionable, somewhat spiked, highlighted hairstyle. Her intense stare burns into me as she tries to decipher questions and to address all possible sides of an issue. Although an activist to the core, Steele is a seasoned and polished negotiator and a successful advocate for her brand of neighborhood community policing. She explains that her desire to establish the first cop shop met initial resistance from the police, for whom such new strategies threatened existing resources. She convinced the police department she would do it all: open the cop shop, staff it, and leave the police out of the picture. With the success of and media attention on Steele's initial shop, police department support followed quickly, including the city's agreement to cover the liability of the COP Shops.

One of Steele's constant struggles remains the east-central location—a predominately minority and lower-income section of the city. At a recent community meeting there to address grievances, the air became so heated, some participants said, that the police chief seethed and walked out. Steele says she tried to convey her message, that "we're not the problem. We're okay. We're not just trying to find what's wrong in neighborhoods, we're also searching neighborhoods for resources: who can garden, who has tools. We're pulling together. Searching for community is the key. I want to do it until collaboration with the city has become part of [residents'] cognitive function." (At the same time, the well-spoken Steele suggests several times that citizens should pull themselves up by their bootstraps and that she wishes she could just make them see what they could do if they "stop killing each other and do for each other.")

Steele can tell one anecdote after another about how she has seen people come back into the fold through COP Shops. She explains how a gang member who had recently been released from jail stopped by the COP Shop and asked whether Steele had seventy-five cents for a bus ride. The former gangster needed the fare to pick up his belongings and move out of town. He wore only a pair of jeans, no shirt, and no shoes, and his body had numerous tattoos. She gave him the seventy-five cents, and he came back later to thank her. Steele believes she established a bridge to the man.

When Steele became the victim of a drive-by shooting—a warning in retaliation for her anticrime activities—the police chief suggested she go to the police academy and learn to handle a gun. She decided against carrying a weapon and instead renewed her faith in neighbors. Like Katherine Anderson, Steele has stories about successes built on this quest for community interdependence. The stories take on a certain magical quality as she tells how the properly informed and mobilized community need not serve a quasipolice function but instead can reduce reliance on formal criminal justice intervention as a viable problem-solving tool.

In one neighborhood, for example, two truant teens were causing problems. The police wanted to call on child-protective services to remove the children from their home, because officers believed that the teens' single mother, who worked, could not properly supervise them. As it turned out, the mother worked an early shift and thought her children were leaving for school each day, but they were actually staying home. When the neighbors heard all the facts at a community meeting, they decided to help out. One sixty-year-old retiree volunteered to pick the teens up at home each morning and escort them to school. Steele points out that making neighbors aware of the problem, followed by a little brainstorming, brought about a solution that pleased everyone involved. The truant teens did not mind the escort—they had not really been trying to miss school so much as they simply had not made an effort to go—and the older neighbor who served as an escort discovered two young friends.

Like Portland's neighborhood associations and coalitions, COP Shops are housed in a variety of locations, from old grocery storefronts to once-decaying homes on busy street corners. The COP Shop Association enters into leases with the city or with the federal Department of Housing and Urban Development, which allows them the use of the properties for one dollar a year while the city pays the utilities. In some cases the shops have received federal community development funds. A weathered Victorian home with cracked clapboard slats and a buckled foundation is undergoing renovation thanks to a $114,000 federal grant.

The shops serve as places for community meetings, field offices for parole and probation officers, and places where neighborhood resource officers come to fill out reports, hold meetings, and receive some pampering. As one volunteer put it, "We look upon the COP Shop as a place where our NRO can come and put his feet up and take a breather." Many COP Shops provide private offices for their NROs. Community members like to bring in snacks and generally make sure their NROs receive proper care.

As my escorts take me from a COP Shop downtown to the problematic COP Shop in east-central Spokane, I count four pawnbrokers on one block. There are signs for space to lease, a bingo parlor, adult bookstores, abandoned vehicles, massage parlors, and ten taverns. We pass car lot after car lot—"gypsy car lots," my escorts call them. Spokane is the home to the president of the gypsy nation, a man who was recently arrested for fencing stolen property. "The police seized one million in cash that had been sewn into quilts and another five hundred thousand in fenced jewelry," one of my escorts explains. As we head through the residential neighborhoods, asbestos-tiled single-family homes with sagging roofs line the streets. A gospel mission stands on a corner, its paint peeling. Near the mission we pass a house with old tires, beds, and carpets in the yard.

My escorts operate a COP Shop in a more affluent section of town. They are two white retirees who have a keen interest in helping in any way they can. They also make sure to let me know about the varying socioeconomic makeup of COP Shop volunteers: "We have some people who can travel to galleries in Europe just to see art and some who have to rub two nickels together just to feel they have some money." Their take on the people they serve in the community is generous: "There are plenty of people living poor, but generally they are good people. Just because they live in some of these areas doesn't mean they have to live that way." "That way" is meant to imply a lifestyle involving illegal behavior.

One method to enable the community to police illegal behavior involves citizens taking part in NOP, an acronym for Neighborhood Observation and Patrol. My escorts believe that their job is welcomed by the law-abiding citizens. Only those choosing to live "that way" yell and call NOP volunteers "nasty old people" when they pass by in their cars, which the police department equips with spotlights and yellow magnetic door placards bearing the NOP emblem.

NOP volunteers are armed with a flashlight and radio, nothing more. "When we first started we were just a bunch of old people," one volunteer recalls. "We can't arrest anybody and we don't have guns. Some guys came in with .357 Magnums and were going to cut crime in half. We had to put a stop to that." The police gave the volunteers training, and now they feel that they make a sizable difference in the areas they patrol. Although they experience verbal harassment on occasion, they see that harassment as a sign that they are doing their job right. Physical retaliation is not a threat, because they believe their close contact with the police gives them power that criminals respect.

In some COP Shops the NRO places problem addresses on a board and NOP keeps the locations under surveillance. The coalition problem-solving routine is similar in Portland. The Portland Police Bureau provides lists of chronic nuisances—ranging from late-night parties and juvenile loitering or drinking, to prostitution and abandoned vehicles—with recommendations about which locations to target for community intervention. The response can take the form of a letter, a phone call, a neighborhood meeting, or the compilation of evidence about offenses.

Some volunteers I meet overtly oppose the NROs' posting hotspot information, some are just not sure it is a good idea, and others do not give the practice much thought. All the volunteers I talk with believe that they are doing the right thing, regardless of the degree of their uneasiness about the potential civil liberty issues raised by posting the addresses of problem locations. As one volunteer tells me, "By the time you are trained, you are so completely involved in what you are doing that you believe in it."

We come upon the East-Central COP Shop, in the lower-income neighborhood that continues to present problems. When the shop was under construction, the roof was firebombed. Bullet holes often appeared on the property, and the windows were smashed. Now wire screens adorn the windows and the building is protected by a steel roof. It is a square, squat fortress of a building, a far cry from the inviting Victorians, old taverns, and empty retail spaces that are headquarters for other neighborhood bases. The shop once housed thirty volunteers, but those numbers are now down to a level insufficient to do any good, according to the shop's liaison. Police come and go, and use the location mainly for report writing. One resident of the area explained how difficult it was to involve herself in the COP Shop because of the fear she felt: "Somebody might come by and shoot my house up." Other issues are also at play, as the resident noted: "I was supposed to speak at a meeting, but by the time I got home from work I couldn't find a baby-sitter and I was too tired to go."

My escorts explain that the most likely perpetrator of the firebombing was a drug dealer who owned a business near the shop. As we leave, we round a corner and pass a building sitting in the middle of all this turmoil. Its windows have no bars on them. Its doors are wide open. This is the site for the Spokane Neighborhood Action Programs. When I contact the director of community services on the phone, I begin to see a world in stark contrast to that of the COP Shops, the NOP, and the volunteers and activists directly linked to quasipolice functions.

Dan Jordan is that director of community services for the Spokane Neighborhood Action Programs, a nonprofit antipoverty agency that oversees programs such as Head Start and school lunches. He explains that the retaliation against the East-Central COP Shop was more troubling than it seemed at first glance, and infinitely more complex. He tells me the economic setting makes it difficult for some individuals to escape a world inhabited equally by scary criminals and crackdown-happy police: "People feel forced, not able to move from the area, and yet the area has become this target for stepped-up police activity. You live in such a state for only so long before you want to do something."

The essential problem, according to Jordan, is that "police want crime to function as a separate issue," but it is too complex a problem to address separately from other social issues. "To really bring about a change in attitude and substantial change in the neighborhood, you need something like a ten-year plan, complete with funding, and it will steamroller as you get more local people involved. Eventually the result will be lower crime, but that's only part of the picture, and you can't just couch it in those terms, because others will be turned off."

For Jordan, the police respond best to middle-class fears and concerns, and they try to orient lower-class concerns around the same issues. "The middle class reacts because they fear they have something to lose, and they feel they are immune to drugs" and to all the problems of the lower class. The middle class, Jordan asserts, aims for quick, reactive strategies. "We should be doing things like asset mapping rather than need surveys. They [the police] shouldn't be coming in to define how bad off you are or what the problems are."

When I tell Jordan that Cheryl Steele emphasizes not just focusing on the bad but also highlighting resources neighborhoods have, he describes a troubling scenario for any resource-hungry program at a time when resources are limited. He explains that at one COP Shop in the eastern part of the city, a prominent volunteer's "hand got caught in the cookie jar." The event brought to light factions split over a number of service-delivery issues. A demarcation developed between residents who supported the police activity in the area and those who had misgivings about it. "There is still not a lot of trust or energy that goes into the east in a positive way," Jordan warns. When I ask what could be done about the impasse, he responds, "They can just start talking. The police are always eyeing some big solution. They don't have to have a solution. They should aim for being creative and forming coalitions."

I began to see just how deep the rift had become between the police department and its COP Shops and some area residents as I gathered more data on the anger and alienation behind the retaliation against the East-Central COP Shop. A well-known and respected community businessman who owns a store close to the shop said that for many residents it was an affront to have "a bunch of old white folk come in and keep tabs on us." He angrily told me, "NOP. You know what that really stands for? Niggers Over-Policed!" He cautioned, "Community policing is working for much of Spokane because it's being waged on the backs of young black males. What program couldn't succeed with such a common and despised enemy in this country?"

When I tell him that many community members support police intervention because they are fed up with gang activity and street-corner drug markets, he remains adamant: "Look, we live it all the time. We live with the crime and we live with the police. I'm not saying we should allow the crime. What I'm saying is, Southside [an affluent neighborhood] has just as much drug dealing, but they can hide it better. You don't see police spending all this time targeting folks up on the hill [in Southside], because they [the residents] have clout. Their kids get to seek treatment. Our kids get prison. So you see, the crime is the same, but the targets are different and the reaction is different."

"You know what that shop was?" He points to the fortress-style COP Shop nearby. "It was a spy shop to a lot of people in this neighborhood. Some people were behind it because they've been told what to do for so long, they just follow whatever's going on. The ones who wanted our people to take care of our own problems, who wanted our men to mentor our boys, they were labeled as sympathetic with the criminals. It's not about being sympathetic with criminals, it's about finding ways for our people to do it. Otherwise it won't mean anything; otherwise you got a bunch of white folk telling us how we should act."

I drive a few blocks away where I meet with Eileen Thomas, another outspoken critic of community policing, the COP Shop, and the current police policies. She is also a member of the Spokane City Human Rights Commission. We converse as she scrambles around her kitchen preparing dinner for her grandchildren and a foster child. Occasionally she yells at her son's dog, which has been barking in the backyard since my arrival. Her home is simple, her kitchen appliances and amenities few and worn. She speaks with eloquence, passion, and almost the same yearning that I heard in Mukilteo's Chief Walters: a yearning for a more collective, more humane, and broader-focused resolution to crime and the problem of criminal behavior; a yearning for a truly civil society where all are invited to participate and none feel alienated. "Community policing is working," she tells me, "but for whom?"

What troubles Thomas the most are the perceptions that COP Shops and the NOP foster with regard to people of color and the young. "It works two ways," she says as she describes an antigang video that the police wanted to show in the high schools. "European Americans see the video, which shows all these young African American men being herded like cattle, these mass arrests, and that's the image they have of us. Our young African American men watch something like that and start to accept this as their fate. For them it's not a scare tactic or deterrent, it's a commentary on the life they will face, and they may even become conditioned to being treated poorly by the police." Thomas waged a last-minute campaign to keep the police from showing the video. She finally succeeded when she called upon the United States Department of Education.

For Thomas, programs designed by the police are merely symbolic and ineffective. They are symbolic in that they either reinforce white stereotypes or ease white fears by conveying a message of massive control over a black threat. They are ineffective because their target audiences, such as teens with Drug Awareness and Resistance Education, live in a world that is far removed from classroom lectures, far from orderly, yet the police seek an ordered, concise management of problems. "You know what the kids tell me DARE means?" Thomas asks. I shake my head. "They tell me it means Drugs Are Really Expensive." I laugh, but there is something important in that sarcastic quip.

There is a joke among my colleagues who study policing that you have to find a good acronym for your theory or program. If you get a good acronym, then you are guaranteed that the program will win acceptance. In the previous chapter we saw a steady stream of acronyms used by Spokane police to name teen intervention programs. Residents in east-central Spokane have shown a clever knack for taking these appealing, mass-marketed acronyms and reshaping them into covert symbols of resistance.

FEAR AND MISTRUST

"Take someone from New York City and drop them down in the middle of Spokane, and they'd laugh how safe it is," Thomas says. "The European Americans just fear us in unbelievable ways!" Her words are not without truth. When I arrived in town, I parked my car on one of the quietest, most peaceful streets I had ever seen—reminiscent of my childhood—to unpack some items. As I unloaded my belongings in the first of several places I would stay, the white host came running to warn me that I had left my car door open. No matter that I was carrying items in and would not leave the car unattended for more than a few seconds; he warned me to keep it locked. On my way to interview people in the east-central district without the aid of my police escorts, another white host at first warned me not to venture into the neighborhood, and then insisted that if I did go I should borrow one of her pepper-spray canisters.

Trust waned and fear from both sides grew. Several black individuals I interviewed would not speak to me until I assured them I would not write down or tape the conversation and would not use their names. There were other uncomfortable moments before I could establish rapport. Eileen Thomas is outspoken, minces no words, and is friendly. I explain some of my work to her, and she retrieves a book from a counter: "I hope you do something like this. We've got to get the message out." I notice that the author of the book is a colleague of mine. I tell her about the coincidence and we quickly develop a genuine and moving rapport. As I prepare to leave, I glance at pictures of her children and she proudly tells me about each.

Her son, she explains, is a football star and into fancy cars. She told him to move to the West Coast because his taste for cars meant that he was constantly being stopped as a person fitting the profile of a drug dealer. "I told him if he didn't leave, he would end up dead sooner or later." I ask her where he has settled, but she moves on to talk about her daughter, either not hearing me or not wanting to answer. Her daughter currently lives in Indiana, and I explain that I did some graduate work in Bloomington. I inquire with genuine curiosity which town her daughter lives in. Again, she does not answer. Despite the rapport we have developed, at the moment I cannot help wondering if she too harbors a mistrust so deep that it operates in subtle, nearly imperceptible ways. As I leave her I watch a neighbor—a white neighbor—bringing a gift-wrapped package to Thomas. Perhaps there is hope.

DESIRE FOR POLITICAL POWER

Can community members join the police when they feel like victims of police abuse? Perhaps not. Then again, when you are involved with police you are involved with power in America. Police provide both mythic power and actual power. For some—the retired professional or the white, middle-class home owner—that power is substantial enough to offer a gratifying and stimulating experience. It provides excitement, a little "in" in a world where knowing someone or something is treasured.

Others, particularly members of the lower class, feel that police power is too frequently used against them; thus, they seldom see it as a problem-solving tool to embrace. In some places, such as Santa

Ana, people weary of police action have initially jumped on the bandwagon, momentarily pacified despite their lack of substantial power. This type of citizen activity may not, however, be what they actually want. For example, a Portland coalition leader who became involved in crime prevention following a neighborhood shooting found that, typically, older residents are more involved and there is less interest among the young and the poor. The activities she promoted in her neighborhood included organizing a safety fair, distributing a list of crime victims, and printing a flyer in Spanish. Still, she seemed dismayed that the young and lower-income people shied away from such neighborhood action.

This leader told me that at one meeting a substantial number of people showed up and took an interest, but their interest was limited to forming a tenants' association to deal with abuses from landlords. Unfortunately, she noted, "there was nothing we could really do. NCPS [Neighborhood Crime Prevention Specialists] could refer them to someone else, but that's about it. There's just so much on our plate to deal with: crime, police, crime prevention, and DARE."

Karen Powell, who runs a different coalition in Portland, also observed that "people want to take a political stance, but this is not the solution offered by the police. The structure offered by the police is limited to begin with, and they tend to still react to problems." Only six neighborhoods in Powell's precinct of thirteen provide any structure for community response with the police. Any direct political voice would be difficult to support and manage.

In Portland's central-southeast neighborhood a large influx of Latinos has brought issues beyond crime to the forefront. In one coalition survey, respondents voiced concerns about cultural events, youth employment, education, services for the mentally ill, and public bathroom facilities. Crime was sixth on the list.

Another issue relates to the extent to which a variety of community members should be available to sit at the discussion table. Can a chief of police manage to control his or her temper to sit through a community meeting in which the police department is not discussed in the most positive light? At most meetings in Portland, the citizens talk first, crime-prevention people next, and the police last. Another problem is that the police are not certain how events such as a multicultural festival will directly affect crime. Their mission is to catch the bad guys, so they constantly try to carry out that mission and, however unintentionally, they reorient community energy in that direction.

$$\approx o \approx$$

According to researchers who have investigated police and community response to drugs and other crimes, police are perhaps the most potent governmental "enablers" of sustained community response. Katherine Anderson's hopeful efforts to deal with hate crime in Portland were dependent on a great many things, including the police helping to bring various parties to the discussion table. Another important factor in addressing bias crime was that Anderson saw herself and her job less as crime fighter and more as community ombudsperson—in other words, as an educator and resource developer, not a police officer. In contrast, in another part of Portland, difficult-to-create-and-maintain community mobilization and power, reflected in the desire to do something about tenants' rights, were discouraged by a predefined notion of what crime control should mean.

The words of Spokane's Dan Jordan have stayed with me, reminding me that the police often want crime to function as a separate issue from other messy and complex issues of contemporary America. At no time is Jordan's observation more evident than when the official crime rates drop. Except for those few brave leaders, such as Sullivan and Walters, who want to focus on the big picture, most will place credit for such drops on some programmatic police invention or on the steadfast lockup of more criminals and the pursuit of harsher sentences. Rarely is a robust economy and low unemployment mentioned as a reason for the latest drop in crime. I do not mean to suggest that economy and employment cause or prevent crime. I do, however, mean to suggest that crime can be seen as part of an ecological picture that may include other community variables, not only those of economics but those pertaining to cultural, moral, symbolic, and perhaps even spiritual life as well.

Understanding this last point allows us to comprehend why issues such as fear and retaliation can occur when police try to

68 inspire community goodwill and crime control through indigenous community power. Fear and retaliation are unintended consequences. Spy shops emerge in a world where a narrowly conceptualized image of crime control exits. "Nasty Old People" and "Drugs Are Really Expensive" become subversions of such otherwise smart-sounding acronyms as NOP and DARE when adults and children are astute enough to know that the issues that concern them are bigger than the neatly packaged schemes designed to help them.

In the quest for the civil and idyllic community, then, police are an important, much-wanted, and necessary ingredient, but so are the community members. Neither can do it alone, and the community cannot partner with the police to carry out only policing functions. The success that Katherine Anderson's story speaks about comes from the police and the community coproducing safety. In this coproduction, each party brings to the table its own special abilities and desires, much like the discussion sessions that occurred in Portland neighborhoods, where listening, overcoming alienation and hurt, and establishing political power were synonymous with "to protect and serve."

4. Incivilities and Shared Conceptions

Is the community project doomed in our culture?

Just because you build a community doesn't mean
everyone in it gets along.
> —Dan Fost, *Marin Independent Journal,*
> July 13, 1997

In his summation on community, Dan Fost reports on a "village-building exercise" that took place on a July weekend in Fairfax, California. Fairfax is a quaint, slightly eccentric bedroom town nestled in the redwood trees midway between San Francisco and Point Reyes. On its streets and in its trendy corner cafés, tie-dye-clad holdouts from the 1960s mingle with harried, cappuccino-sipping soccer moms. The Campaign for a Healthier Community for Children sponsored the exercise, in which children built their own village out of cardboard. The observers, volunteers from a world peace center, nonprofit schools, and parents, offered as little assistance as possible, preferring instead to sing songs and tack up peace banners.

As Fost tells it, the children soon began transforming the cardboard into "swords, guns and missiles." One seven-year-old girl told Fost that "these kids are making like a war place and if people go in, they'll hit them." So a brother and a sister quickly built a village jail. Two older boys constructed a missile silo and a bazooka. Upon seeing the arms race in the children's peace village, one of the adult organizers asked Fost, "I wonder how much of that is innate human nature?" According to Fost, "It took a group of children to teach adults the law of human nature."

In the introduction I raised the supposition that some magical quality is indigenous to communities and that only this quality can ultimately and adequately solve social ills, thus reducing the need for state intervention. I highlighted a symbolic desire for a communal, humane lifestyle in places such as Mukilteo and Spokane. I pointed to a desire for community-based strategies to deal with social ills in those and other places even if, in practice, such strategies often fail to materialize fully.

In Santa Ana, Spokane, and Portland, I found that poor and minority residents seemed to show little concern for their neighborhoods, but I then learned that they have different views regarding important problems to address. Because building community can help control crime and because the police represent the most immediately conceptualized crime-control tool, I first looked at how town leaders, police officers, and citizens working with police struggled to create community by relying on the criminal justice enterprise. Their efforts have been hamstrung, I surmised, because a system that uses the threat of arrest makes for a poor community builder. It can too readily create divisions along race and class lines and disrupt already fragile inner-city ecologies.

In this chapter I begin to examine other ways in which community is hampered or facilitated. Irrespective of the extent of police programs, I conclude that any community project will require a shared consensus on public behavior if it is going to succeed. The Fairfax village war, however, suggests alternative views: shared cultural conceptions have little bearing on behavior; police and jails are necessary components of any system dealing with human nature; differences along class and racial lines are part of human nature, as are poor moral faculties; and community builders must contend with the uneasy realization that some people in a community just will not get along with everyone else.

I am tempted to discount such alternative views, seeing them as more evidence of the attribution error mentioned in chapter 1. This, after all, was a common refrain in the early part of the twentieth century: The unclean and uncivilized masses who lack moral stature do things that bother us. We need to educate them and impress upon them the need for what the movement at the time called "social hygiene." Women first entered policing in the 1920s during the age of Prohibition, a time when moral campaigns were in high gear, precisely because female Victorian virtues were thought to help create "hygiene" and to bring order to bawdy city establishments. Women officers were charged with approving liquor licenses, checking on entertainment venues, and enforcing a host of moral-order laws.

Nowadays police in some areas protect "beat health." Such efforts are designed to check on problem locations for physical incivilities, graffiti, vandalism, and broken windows. The difference between "hygiene" and "beat health" is one of magnitude. Whereas the social hygiene movement sought to reform individuals and make them more "middle-class," the new beat-health concept enjoins communities to focus on reducing trash, graffiti, and other signs of disorder thought to precipitate crime in run-down neighborhoods. As much as I want to disregard the claims of the moralists and Fost's warning that the Fairfax exercise reveals the darker side of human nature, I need to contend with some very troubling experiences encountered during my own travels. They are experiences that tell me the community project faces a tough, uphill battle if it is going to embrace all the members of a community, especially when those members exhibit bothersome incivilities, as sociologists call them, that can make many of us uncomfortable and fearful.

CLASSES DIVIDED

My battle to embrace community visions begins on a weekend day during a five-day stay with an Arizona parole officer and his wife, a dispute resolution specialist. We have been languishing in Tempe and Phoenix all week, driving the mean and not-so-mean streets, talking about crime, criminals, and other criminal justice issues. The day is not unusually hot for Arizona, but the parole officer (whom I'll call Jason) and I decide to take a break and head for Canyon Lake to do some swimming.

As we approach the lake, rain clouds fill the sky to the south. To the east a red-gray haze hangs over Phoenix. Jason tells me this is smog. The long, straight interstate, framed by minimalls, commercial parks, and gravel-strewn fields, eventually turns to a winding, hilly highway surrounded by Arizona's familiar cactus and red-soil desert. We drive for another forty minutes or so and come upon the lake, nestled in a narrow canyon. We begin looking for a spot to dive off rocks and are directed by some visitors to a main picnic area down the road. As we proceed down the drive, the natural beauty of the lake is disrupted by the thunderous roar of speed-boat engines. White and silver reflections glint from the shore, and I soon notice they come from trash: beer cans, bottles, Styrofoam plates and cups, plastic grocery bags, and empty cardboard beer boxes.

As we make our way into the parking area at the end of the entrance road, we are passed by a pickup truck with four young men sitting in the back. They all wear bathing suits. One man is sporting a sidearm strapped at his waist over red swim trunks. Jason informs me that wearing a weapon is not illegal in Arizona as long as it is in plain view and the owner carries a permit. I mumble something to Jason to the effect that swimming must be dangerous business these days, and we continue on. I remember that in Spokane concealed weapons are legal and are commonly carried. In fact, the people I met shared considerable weapons-related information with their friends: who carried what, how they obtained permits, where they wore their guns.

In the parking lot proper, a sunburned, seemingly drunk man stumbles from the driver's seat of his pickup truck and urinates alongside the cab, his urine splattering the pavement with a quick sizzle in the hot sun. Park bathrooms stand empty no more than fifty feet away. Finally at the water's edge, we wade past trash that forms a foot-wide rim along the shore. We contemplate crossing over a small channel to a diving rock. I decide I want to sit and take in more of this world I am encountering, so Jason swims over without me. While I watch him dive off a small cliff, several youngsters play in the rocks lining the shore. Their father, his back a sun-painted red, keeps a close watch. To my right, a woman and a man sit drinking beer and talking. Jason dives off an even higher precipice, and my attention turns again to the woman on my right. She has now launched into a full verbal tirade at her partner, because he has somehow spotted her shirt with mud. Her words are laced with every possible profanity. Ten feet away the children stop playing and stare. Their father looks disturbed. Jason swims back over to me. I tell him that I need to find a place without so many people if I am truly going to relax.

On the drive back to Tempe, the rain finally reaches our stretch of the road. A squall spreads across the ridges to the west, and the desert is cleansed. A rainbow arcs over one end of the valley. The desert, as harsh a climate as it is, offers a peaceful atmosphere compared to the one at the lake. I want to be more forgiving. I want to embrace those people. But even if reaching out and developing more interdependent relations may help address political problems, may cross many hurdles, and may bring resolution to social crises, I am at a loss as to how to reach those people at Canyon Lake. My disgust is too great. My snobbishness at what Jason and I refer to as "white trash" when we later tell the story to his wife is too profound. Does the problem rest with me, with them, or with all of us?

I chose the term "white trash" to describe the visitors we saw at Canyon Lake before I read a guidebook on Portland, Oregon. Prior to their gentrification, the same neighborhoods in which Katherine Anderson and her neighborhood coalition dealt valiantly with hate crime had been referred to as Portland's "white trash enclave." Later, when I call Jason to ask permission to use the information about him for this chapter, I talk again about the lake trip. Jason's wife tells me, "You should have been with us when we went tubing the other week. At the end of the trip we were making our way toward the shore, and we saw all these pickup trucks and Blazers parked along the shore. Nothing but trucks. Then we saw these three guys standing in the water, drinking beer, and holding a sign, a big sign." On the other phone line Jason interjects, "It was the size of a sheet of plywood." His wife incredulously describes the sign: "They had painted on it, 'Show ye rack.'" Jason laughs at the sign writer's effort at cleverness in using the Old English "ye." His wife tells me that some women in rafts and tubes were obliging the men's request.

On another leg of my trip, on another river, with other friends—this time in Sacramento, California—I came across similar sights.

On the South Fork of the American River one hot afternoon, as in the primal journey in *Heart of Darkness,* it seemed that we encountered every conceivable disturbance.

On that day, boaters were drunk and cursed with abandon. One boatload of teens was so drunk that several members had to disembark so they could vomit in bushes along the shoreline. Further downriver, a man in an inflatable kayak had mounted a portable stereo on his raft, positioning two large speakers on the gunwale, and was assaulting the area with Lynard Skynard and AC/DC. For some, I suppose he was a moving concert hall. I started to describe the scene I had witnessed in Arizona for my hosts, a public defender and his wife. They both stopped my disparaging analysis dead in its tracks by proclaiming that they loved this river and that the experience we were getting was first-rate democracy. The public defender took a deep breath as if to inhale the putrid but life-giving scent this type of democracy offers. There was some truth to what he said. The incivilities were not an immediate physical threat, and when I considered the public defender's analysis of them I was not morally outraged. Perhaps there was something to this democracy. Perhaps my repulsion was just a product of my own snobbishness.

Outside the courthouse in Spokane on another hot summer day, I sat waiting for an interview. I decided to take notes on the people coming and going on the courthouse steps. There were the office workers, the sheriff's deputies, and a steady stream of employees leaving the building to smoke cigarettes. Then there were the people who came for court business. Invariably they all fit nicely into a stereotype that loudly spoke about "class." I felt they all underdressed for their court appearances. One man wore high-top sneakers, shorts, and a tank top. Another sported a cowboy hat, dirty blue jeans, and a Western shirt. A woman hustled past me in a Mickey Mouse sweatshirt and sweatpants. One man, looking completely drunk, sat on the court steps trying to gain some composure, his face flushed in the morning heat. Finally he stood, staggered up the steps, caught himself against a pillar, and entered the building. Two sheriff's deputies stood in an alley, smoking cigarettes and laughing at the drunk.

I could not help thinking that these people were putting themselves at a disadvantage. No matter how blind justice is supposed to be, the stereotype they portrayed would stay with them throughout their court appearance—not to mention that it may have already *contributed to* their court appearance. A nice suit can go a long way toward making a judge and court clerks treat a visitor with more respect, but these people were not giving themselves that opportunity. Could they not afford nicer clothes? Could they not borrow something? Did they care? Did they even know? I guessed they did not. I cautioned myself that some people, through learning and life-style, just may not understand how minor details such as littering, venturing into public wearing guns strapped to their hips, urinating in parking lots, or showing up for court in sweats affect their social interaction. Such behaviors are just the way they do things.

SHAPING WHAT WE DO

My public defender friend and his wife would have us exuberantly uphold the boundless mix of behavior that takes place in our communities. As long as none of this behavior presents physical danger to us, then we should see it for what it is: a price we pay for living in a democracy. The onus on those of us who feel threatened by people who behave differently from us is to "get over it." This logic is persuasive in that it engenders greater tolerance and it does not defend one "right" behavior over others. Unfortunately, however, where incivilities exist, crime flourishes. In 1990, Wesley Skogan, a professor of political science and urban affairs, published findings from his methodologically complex reanalysis of neighborhood and crime-related data from forty cities in the United States. Time and again Skogan found that as physical incivilities increased in neighborhoods, so too did behavioral incivilities, and that as both increased, crime and fear of crime also escalated in a feedback loop.

This is not to say that relying on "collective efficacy" and the indigenous abilities found in communities will depend on enforcing some static moral code. Rather, such a reliance will have to come from the way people actually do things. If as a reporter or a parent we watch children destroy a cardboard village that is supposed to teach shared values and establish community cohesion, we might say it is just human nature that many of our fellow citizens do not conceptualize modes of behavior from the standpoint of the community. But we need not stop there. This book is based on a narrative of observation and reflection, but science is the guide that can help decipher what the eyes see and what the mind thinks. When I turn to science for some relief, I begin to understand that the incivilities I witnessed may be due to some other variable, such as the social network to which people are tied, from which they pick up the resources and experiences that shape their public behavior.

A popular belief in American culture is that one method to shape the way people do things is to educate those people, as was exemplified during the social hygiene movements. The next three chapters examine strategies for shaping the way people do things that depend first on the physical environment, next on social mixing, and then on legal codes. The intent is to highlight that the cardboard guns and jails in Fairfax and the apparently drunk, urinating park visitor in Arizona are not mere reflections of human nature. Individuals can and do respond to their culture in a constant process of shaping and creating conceptualizations based on all facets of their life and the environment.

Jason, the parole officer who supervises clients in Chandler's and Tempe's worst neighborhoods, simplified this analysis in a useful way. One evening as we passed from a drab, deteriorated neighborhood into a more colorful, commercially successful district, he told me, "You can tell which ones [parolees] will make it on the outside and which ones won't simply by the addresses where they get paroled to. You can map it out. The ones who are paroled in that area back there [the run-down neighborhood] will probably reoffend. The ones on this side, they got a good chance."

Although focusing on individual attributes may seem sufficient in an age marked by rugged individualism, such a focus overlooks a central characteristic of human behavior: humans are social beings who respond constantly to social processes and environments, because such response carries a distinct survival advantage. In their thorough examination of the literature on cognitive processes from pigeons and rats to humans and human societies as a whole, Ervin Laszlo and his colleagues tell us in *Changing Visions,* "As members of societies, people will do to varying degrees what the social system wants, not what they want to do themselves." The simple but evocative examples used by Laszlo et al. are sports, disasters, and wars. In sports, teammates will work harder as a team than each member could do on his own. In disasters, citizens who might ordinarily show little interest in civic affairs will serve in fire brigades, pile sandbags, and direct traffic. During wars, soldiers will risk life and limb for their unit, but they may retreat to a solitary lifestyle when the war is over. This does not mean that such responses are unique to intense events. What it means is that those specific settings or occurrences differ so much from day-to-day existence that individual behavior as it is influenced by the group is clearly discernible.

Laszlo and his colleagues tell us that the root of the social response is the human thinking process. Despite IBM's best efforts to prove otherwise, there is no more efficient information processor than the human brain. It maintains the capacity to respond to a new environment in unique ways, depending on the cues, or feedback mechanisms, in that environment. This efficient and powerful tool requires humans to "think" quite differently than a computer does. A computer checks information by a one-to-one correspondence with what exists in its memory. For example, a computer might interpret the following command as a way to distinguish one piece of tableware from another:

Silver + metal + sharp edge + one edge + handle = knife.

Humans, however, examine their environment by a representation of wholes, or what perceptual scientists call the gestalt of the information in their memory as contexualized by the environment. Thus, as Laszlo and his colleagues suggest, an object on the kitchen counter most likely fits into the context of the kitchen: a knife, a can opener, a fork. Although the object on the counter may in fact be a pipe wrench, for the most part human survival is well served by this representational mapping: "It is easier for the brain to deal with a solid living tiger than to consider separately the implications of its odor, its stripes, its roar, and so on!"

Improved computer modeling of complex variables that represent the ecology of a community, a neighborhood, or a residential block has helped clarify how contexts are embedded with cues, much like a kitchen, and how these contexts can bring about certain social behaviors. As Skogan reminds us, a context rife with social incivilities begets more of the same. These contexts can exist on a local level, as in an inner-city neighborhood, or more globally, as with the children in Fairfax who mirrored a culture's reliance on war tools and jails in shaping communities.

Efforts to reshape contextual cues to prevent crime usually entail citizens banding together to change the look of their neighborhoods or to provide neighborhood watch groups. As I have demonstrated in previous chapters, however, the effectiveness of such efforts often falls along class lines. Skogan notes in *Disorder and Decline* that "relying upon voluntary local organizations to deal with disorder and crime places poorer communities at a disadvantage relative to middle-class areas." Those poorer communities seldom independently start, carry through, or maintain any collective efforts because of their transient populations.

As a whole, community action occurs less frequently among those who need it most—the disadvantaged. These are the findings presented by Sidney Verba and a group of colleagues in the *American Political Science Review.* Verba's team used a national survey of households in 1989 to determine who participates in American democracy and for what reasons. As the economic continuum shifted from the advantaged (those who owned homes and were financially secure) to the needy (those who experienced some financial hardship) to those receiving means-tested benefits, participation dropped for all activities. These activities included contacting public officials, attending protests, being active at community meetings, serving on a local board, or working campaigns.

In the *Journal of Social Issues,* Douglas Perkins, Barbara Brown, and Ralph Taylor explain that people who pursue grassroots responses to social problems benefit from access to resources and usually rely on institutions such as churches and a high degree of neighboring. In survey data taken from studies in Utah, New York, and Maryland, Perkins and his colleagues did not find very strong evidence that community organizing was motivated by fears, perceptions of crime, or victimization. Although such activity may prove important for motivating leaders (as is demonstrated in chapter 3), in the aggregate it does not go a long way toward promoting community problem solving.

What does work, according to Perkins et al., is collective "community-focused cognition and behaviors." In other words, a solidarity and cohesion based on a conception that values informal sharing promotes the activism needed to respond to problems, the definition of which, in turn, is based on a shared representation of a stable social existence. That stable social existence neither depends on moral upbringing nor, conversely, is threatened by criminal inclination. It is far too dynamic. More than likely, it is dependent on what Ralph Taylor calls "behavior settings." These in turn are shaped by a host of physical, spatial, and cultural variables ranging from the level of the block to that of the nation. Laszlo and his colleagues define a similar setting as a "societal cognitive map," which is a "set of shared symbols describing a collective environment and prescribing the organized behaviors appropriate to preserving social stability in that environment."

One of Skogan's main themes in *Disorder and Decline* is that perhaps the biggest task facing America as it wrestles with crime is to find a common definition for disorder and urban decay. In some communities, multicolored murals and visually busy commercial signs provide popular and continuous cultural expression. Manicured lawns and streets lined with No Parking signs are the expressions of other communities. A ready process that allows for shaping new and stable cognitive settings or maps does not exist. In a later chapter I examine how some people hope the law will achieve this in the future, but the aim here is to define a cognition or shared conception about culturally shaped public behavior as things currently exist.

WHAT WE SHARE

What powerful conception of public behavior do most Americans experience and share? Certainly there is not a clear shared solidarity in Canyon Lake, Arizona, or—unless Americans are as forgiving and optimistic as my friend the public defender—on the South Fork of the American River in California. In my travels exploring the desire for community, I found only one type of place where the social space was clearly defined and where few of its users complained. In this place a shared purpose permeated the environment, and a shared ethos created civilities that were, for the most part, similar across race, class, and age. It was not a community constructed by the police or neighborhood activism. It was a community symbolically built around a powerful American ethos based on consumption. It was the shopping mall.

As Americans, we may not hold a common belief in building community or in sharing with neighbors unless we are compelled by a disaster. We may not all agree on what constitutes community activism or community crime control. We may not all agree on the extent to which multicolored murals are art or graffiti. Few Americans spend a sizable portion of our leisure time "good-neighboring" or trying to establish new relations. Most of us, however, spend considerable leisure time shopping, thinking about shopping, and making plans to acquire more money so we can continue to shop and consume. We do not share a common cognition about informal problem solving as much as we do about informal consumption. The malls have become the perfect community successes, where most people understand their roles and most oblige.

In Indianapolis I visited a mall early one weekday morning with a criminologist. Pointing to a set of lockers at one end of the mall and a steady stream of elderly people in walking and running shoes, she explained that these were "mall walkers." The mall offered them a safe, temperature-controlled, contained environment where they could exercise and visit with others their own age. In Spokane I followed a young dad, his son, and his son's friend on their daily trip to the mall to browse in some stores, to buy a snack, and to visit. They pointed to a blue haze hanging over one end of the mall and told me this was where smokers were allowed. In that haze teenagers gathered, flirted, and checked out their looks. Parents with children, older adults walking hand in hand, and nonsmokers negotiated the smokers. The mall-goers seemed to understand their roles.

In Baltimore I accompanied a policy analyst to a once economically struggling, crime-ridden area of town that had been transformed into a model for waterfront malls. The crowds were thick, the incivilities limited. Those at the mall represented a heterogeneous mix—young and old, black and white, single and married. In Orange County, California, I toured a $55 million theme-styled mall surrounded by obsessively planned housing developments that were populated by predominately white, middle- to upper-class home owners. The mall's extensive marketing research revealed that its visitors came from far beyond the population bordering its parking lots, and from all age, socioeconomic, and race groups.

Jet magazine reported in 1996 that among racial groups, blacks may suffer alarming rates of poverty and may live in areas of serious urban decay, but they have considerable buying power. The average black household spends only fifty dollars less in clothing annually than the average white household. Blacks outspend whites by 10 percent on clothing for children and by 48 percent on food prepared at home. Moreover, "black households spent $10.8 billion in 1995 on new cars and trucks, which [was] a 156 percent increase from the year before." Black dollars keep malls alive as well as white dollars do. Although *Jet*'s intention was to recognize blacks as a powerful market segment that companies ought not to ignore, the report also suggests to me that blacks have the wealth and resources to revitalize their own neighborhoods and communities. Their failure to do so lies less with their lack of motivation or good intentions and more with what economist Mark Sagoff sees as a growing world-cultural paradigm in which commerce has become the means to the end. "We consume too much," Sagoff warns in the *Atlantic,* "when market relationships displace the bonds of community, compassion, culture, and place."

At a mall in Arizona, when I purchased a shirt from an Eddie Bauer store, the too-friendly salesperson handed me a bag that read, "Revisit your childhood, play hooky." I looked at the bag and then at the shoppers around me and thought about the message conveyed by both the bag and the mall. It was the middle of the day. Who were all these people? Were they playing hooky from their jobs, their neighborhoods, their homes? Would their presence at any of those places instead of the mall provide better guardianship or some stability?

If parking lots, lakes, rivers, and our own neighborhoods do not provide cues for civil behavior, then perhaps malls have captured and concentrated them, just as they have concentrated everything else: spending, time, goals, and capital improvements. I probably would have more success, and certainly more comfort, approaching a neighbor at the mall than on my own block. The concern of a community project should remain focused on activities that the mall does not reach: finding communality among neighbors' differences; creating a civil and community sense of meaning; exploring situations that encourage us to share and to solve problems mutually; shaping a world where people know one another. To construct this world like another mall would be to overlook an ecological problem requiring a solution more complex than spatial and physical determinants can provide.

Despite the popular belief that a governmental agency such as the police can fashion shared meaning, the problem defies police strategy and tactics. The reality is that crime is merely a symptom. The search for community must go beyond the symptom toward a realization that may require us to question the way a culture represents itself and to encourage new paradigms for that representation.

≈ o ≈

There is much talk these days about the need for a civil society, about individuals taking responsibility for their communities, and about collaborations geared toward shifting values to improve safety and prevent violence. This talk is not merely polemical. It is now clear that a definite link between incivilities and crime exists. Our feelings of satisfaction with our quality of life and safety in our neighborhoods may depend more on how those around us act than on all the well-intentioned policing money can buy and all the tough laws legislatures can enact.

The facile explanation of incivility continues down a road about differences, claiming that those who feel threatening to us—who upset our balance and demean our quality of life—lack some moral component or perhaps are just geared toward wanton incivility. Science, paired with the stories I have presented thus far, redirects our path to suggest an alternative explanation. Who among us can claim emancipation from the carpetbagging sins of the consumer culture? Who among us will pass up the megamall and the superdiscount warehouse to pay higher prices at a locally owned hardware store or drugstore?

These seemingly benign actions speak to us on two levels. First, our collective actions remind us that we are part of a larger cultural moment that weakens the bonds of communities and has the potential to erode the economic resilience of local ecologies. Second, as part of the consumer narrative we begin to believe we can build and buy the comfort and security we seek: witness the Disney Corporation now building entire towns. In the next two chapters I explore whether it is possible to manufacture community by relying less on people power and more on bricks and paint.

Up to this point I have examined the reliance of the police on people and the dependence of people power on police enabling. The good news is that we can and do share some very powerful and common modes of behavior in our often frenzied consumer dance. Unfortunately, though, these are not the types of behavior likely to create a sense of security and to bolster community cohesion. The stories I have told describe a schism in community that is really a separation of people who represent different classes, races, and values. Finding a way back to the community table still remains a formidable obstacle.

I am reminded how deep this separation can be and how suddenly it can arise as I take a window view of the world from a train heading north to Massachusetts from Baltimore. The train passes a park near Hartford, Connecticut. From my vantage point the world of the park appears neatly boxed, as if in a diorama. A nervous man rushes from a shelter and passes a bag to another equally nervous man who offers money. A drunk stumbles across a lawn. A homeless person lies crumpled on a bench. Three teen boys hop a fence to play basketball. The people I see outside the window are like actors whose stage changes with each passing block. Several blocks along, the train passes an even more dilapidated section of town. A man crouched behind an old couch in a vacant lot watches a women enter a parked car. In that instant my mind thinks the worst. Two blocks farther, families are seated on front stoops on this overcast, humid summer evening, oblivious both to the scene my mind has envisioned two blocks back and to the actors on the stage just around the corner ahead. In another two blocks, five young kids chase a boy on a bicycle down a street that parallels the train tracks.

As if on a theme-park ride, the train crosses a river toward still another diorama window. Framed by a gray, overcast sky, a greener-than-green, perfectly manicured lawn is surrounded by a high chain-link fence and illuminated by a row of light standards. In the fading daylight, young women at a prep school play field hockey in plaid skirts, knee-high socks, and navy blue sweaters.

For an instant my mind envisions a new, encouraging story: I see the field surrounded by the houses with people on the stoops. The kids chasing the bicycle run across a public section on the green field. The field hockey players have stopped for a moment to watch the woman who now safely enters her parked car. For an instant, I see a community with shared concerns and values. For an instant, the conceptual pipe wrench that Laszlo and colleagues talked about is not out of place in the kitchen.

5. Scene of the Crime

Designing space to evoke prosocial community behavior

A state is not a mere society, having a common place,
established for the prevention of mutual crime and for
the sake of exchange. . . . Political society exists for the
sake of noble actions, and not mere companionship.

—Aristotle, *Nicomachean Ethics*

There is a line from the movie *The Hudsucker Proxy* that comically captures the paradox faced by popular place-oriented and order-maintenance crime-control strategies. Hudsucker Industries is controlled by a ruthless and greedy corporate tyrant who concocts a scheme to profit from his own company's demise by appointing a young, simpleminded clerk to succeed him as president. The clerk has his own plan to rejuvenate Hudsucker's failing fortunes, based on an idea so cockamamy (it is a sketch of a circle) that the corrupt company board appoints him unanimously. What his sketch develops into, however, is the hula hoop, an invention that sends Hudsucker's shares skyrocketing. A hard-nosed, intrepid female reporter, who goes undercover to get the scoop on the boy-wonder president, muses about the hula hoop: "Finally there'd be a thing in America that brought people together—even if it kept them apart spatially."

The idea that a thing, some physical element—a fountain, walkway, patio, fence, light standard, or garden—might bring us together socially is an evocative strategy but not one without complications. I begin to explore this strategy by considering an unspeakable crime that took place on a cool afternoon in Middle America in winter's final days, as a once pristine light snow began to melt, forming dark, muddy slush on sidewalks and in street gutters.

The crime shocks the mind not so much because a group of young boys savagely beat a middle-aged woman in the middle of the day on a quiet, tree-lined street. The embarrassment comes from what did not happen. Two neighbors watched and did nothing. A man walking his dog did stop and end the beating, but the police were never called. Reports were never made. Parents were never informed. Citizens were never mobilized. Not that any of those interventions might have changed things. But I can entertain the hope that the community might have done more, that it might have found a way to reconnect the residents in order for some positive action to transcend the brutality: some noble action amid the savageness.

I view the next few minutes through the eyes of Bill, the only person who took action that afternoon. Bill has ventured outside into the chilly air to walk his dog and to smoke a cigar. He is in his mid-twenties, is white, college-educated, and physically assertive, but is not an impressively big person. As he turns a corner, he sees several teenage boys farther down the block yelling epithets at a middle-aged woman standing on her porch. The woman returns the insults, screaming, "You broke my window; now I'm going to break yours!" Across the street two men tend to chores at their respective houses. One washes a car, the other cleans his yard. Bill will later tell me that from the familiarity used in the name-calling, it appeared that a long-standing feud had existed between the youths and the woman. Bill recognizes one boy as the local newspaper carrier. He assumes that the boy might have thrown the paper improperly, prompting the neighbor to yell at him from the porch.

In the next few moments, as Bill moves closer to the scene, the yelling escalates to throwing muddy, slushy snowballs. Who threw what first seems unimportant. Acting on some swift, unspoken command, the youths move in concert, stomping across the slush in the yard and rushing the woman. They grab her, drag her flailing body off the porch through the brown mush, and deposit her in an icy, muddy puddle in the street. They surround her and kick her as she rolls into a fetal position to protect her body from their blows.

The two men tending to chores barely look up. Bill races toward the group, yelling at the boys to stop. The youths back off as he arrives at their side. The woman quickly struggles to her feet and retreats inside. The teens then turn their anger toward Bill. The apparent leader of the group warns Bill to mind his own business or they will "cap" him, and then tries to enlist the other boys in an assault on Bill. The moment is tense. Bill's heart races. Brazenly, perhaps foolishly, he faces them. In what he will later call his best Clint Eastwood, with cigar still clenched firmly in his teeth, he moves an inch or two closer. His body language warns them that he is willing to "bring it on." Only when they are faced with the prospect that ganging up on Bill will also mean that Bill will probably get in a few good licks, the boys decide to back down. The leader follows Bill down the block, trying to generate support for his intended assault, but the steam is gone from his orders. The paperboy returns to his sacks and resumes delivery. The other boys shuffle off. High noon in the plains is over, and the hero walks off into a cold, early spring evening.

There is a further story behind this tale. It happens that Bill is a friend of mine who is in this same line of work, this figuring-out-crime business. Bill knows better than anyone about the need for wider intervention in an event like this, yet he did nothing more than intervene in the immediate situation. I know him so well that I could grill him on every detail and I call him an idiot for not doing more.

I first heard about the incident only hours after it had happened. On the phone with Bill, I tried to explain that the boys did not have any feedback about how their actions were intolerable. Who should have given them that feedback? The neighbors? Their parents? All they received from Bill was a physical intervention that they viewed as inappropriate and considered threatening enough that they wanted to "cap" him. This incident was symptomatic. Something terribly wrong in that neighborhood took place. Those boys crossed the thin line between civilization and anarchy. Bill was the professional. It was up to him to do something. What about the victim? Did anyone even know whether she was okay? My prodding and questioning continued until I thought I had convinced Bill to do something more. Certainly I would have done something more. I would have called the newspaper and informed the management about the carriers they employed. I would have made the police visit each of the youngsters and let his parents know what type of boy they were raising. I would have told the neighborhood what type of neighbors it has, men who wash their cars and tend their yards as crime occurs in front of them.

It was easy for me to think about doing more, sitting two thousand miles away in a warm bungalow on a sunny late afternoon along the California coast. In the moment of the incident, my friend Bill had to contend with the reaction that his action would provoke. After all, in the complex and sometimes confounding study of crime, Bill, like me, knows that sometimes doing something more is doing something worse. When the system intervenes, positive results do not always follow. Calling the newspaper might result in the carrier's termination, which might make him bitter and destabilize his economic resources. Phoning the police might result in arrests and in the juveniles' detention, but there is no guarantee that police intervention would help the boys find better ways to approach future run-ins with this neighbor. Telling neighbors about the boys and about their fellow neighbors' less-than-praiseworthy behavior might create tension and anger in the neighborhood. It probably would change the neighborhood little and would not encourage those noble actions only Bill took.

There is a more important issue as well. The same impulse that brought Bill to intervene, that made a reluctant hero out of him, did not necessarily require him to do more. Whose responsibility was it, after all? What about the victim? She certainly could have called the police. Chances are, the picture was complicated by the fact that the victim was a little crazy, the neighborhood kook. The boys were a bit rambunctious, the neighborhood troublemakers. The two uninterested men probably had seen it before and will see it again. These are not excuses for the crime but a recognition that complex situations do not lend themselves to easy responses. Bill, though threatened himself and greatly disturbed by what he saw, wanted just to move on lest he create even greater trouble. Far removed in California, I wanted the community to regain some stability.

As it turns out, about a week later Bill was jogging and saw the boys hanging out at a local convenience store. To his credit, inspired by the sermon I had pitched, he stopped, calmly sat down next to the boys, and did try to give them the feedback he believed they needed. He started to ask them if they realized what they had done. He wanted to talk to them about solving disputes in a more constructive manner. The boys moved away and ran off.

DETERMINANTS FOR NEIGHBORS' CARE

The last chapter explored the notion that in talk about community projects, the issues that concern Americans may be less about assuaging their fears and controlling crime with massive force, and more about feeling the cooperative sense, a sense of shared values, that fellow Americans can trust one another. They may desire to turn to one another when needed and to share a common conception about the need for prosocial action and proper behavior in social settings. That is, they may desire to form an interdependent community. Scientists who study game theory would submit as much. People are most secure when the behaviors of those around them are predictable and cooperative. Deviations in behavior do not threaten others so long as those who act in a deviant way are willing to cooperate and to do their fair share in a system based on cooperative strategy. A society can exist with less cooperative behaviors, but evolutionary biologists Robert Boyd and Peter Richerson tell us that "because economic and military success require a high degree of interdependence, cooperative cultures will tend to persist longer than less cooperative cultures."

"Culturally endogamous" groups, such as fraternal organizations, academic disciplines, corporations, and kinship networks provide the most powerful means for teaching shared behavior and hence offer the most predictability. Persons in these groups can assume that each other member shares a set of similar values and characteristics. I noted in the last chapter that Wesley Skogan sees in our current cultural climate a world that offers few clear messages as to what are appropriate cooperative behaviors and what are symbolic representations of despised uncooperative conduct. Boyd and Richerson explain how learning behavior, such as cooperation, is frequency-dependent, meaning it must occur in many contexts, many times, and with many actors with whom we come in contact. Thus, it is deceptive to think that we can produce and diffuse such an important cultural conception by relying on the criminal justice system's narrow range of options aimed at a narrow section of the population: people who demonstrate an even more narrow set of antisocial behaviors that we are trying to correct. The criminal justice system plays a minor part in a large equation. If my friend Bill wanted those boys' behavior to change, he was right in not focusing solely on the boys themselves. Unfortunately, even if he had wanted to do more, there was no structure that would have allowed him to address the problem that occurred in that heartland neighborhood.

In our idyllic community replete with indigenous problem solving, we want angry young boys to know how to approach appropriate arbiters to deal with their grievances against kooky neighbors. We want our neighbors to intervene when our safety is in danger but not when our privacy or lifestyle is at issue. We want parents to ensure that their children are corrected but not treated severely. We want some entity (so far, I have assumed it to be the police) to make sure that structures needed to encourage all of these behaviors are in place and are continually used.

Psychologist Elliot Aronson examined situational determinants that lead to intervention and concluded that people who share a common fate are more likely to become involved in helping one another. Aronson reminds us that in 1964 the American public was shocked to learn that thirty-eight New Yorkers stared from their windows and watched for thirty minutes as an attacker savagely stabbed Kitty Genovese to death. The news portrayed the worst that New York had come to represent: alienation, anonymity, urban disorder. Aronson suggests that when we see someone in pain, we can choose to remove ourselves psychologically from doing anything by excusing ourselves from responsibility. In Bill's case, perhaps the apathetic neighbors justified their actions by saying to themselves, "That's the neighborhood kook; she had it coming. Boys will be boys. Someone else is doing something about it." An alternative action begins when we feel empathy for the person in pain and want to do something to assist her. We are most likely to feel empathy when we share some commonality with or have developed an interdependent relationship with the victim.

As I examine a climate that might have brought about more prosocial actions in Bill's neighborhood, it is necessary to expand on the range of methods known to transmit cultural messages, to include variables typically seen as benign. When we discuss cultural representations, we immediately think in capacious terms about common definitions of culture: television, advertising, art, education. In the last chapter I illustrated culture as a period of time marked by certain profound commonalities. In this sense, many elements in our day-to-day experience form a structure that can play a role in precipitating certain behaviors. Altering the very scene of the crime, as it turns out, is a currently popular manifestation of the community project designed to produce "eyes on the street," "territoriality," "informal guardianship," "identity," and other protective, prosocial action. Before I get there, however, it may be helpful to understand where our culture has been.

THE PARADOX OF PLACE

I am on a visit to Bill's heartland neighborhood where the attack on his neighbor took place. My goal is to recognize every possible element in the neighborhood as a potential variable in the criminal event, but I do not ask the usual questions. I do not begin with the kids or their families. I make no effort to learn about the personalities of the do-nothing neighbors across the street from the victim or, for that matter, the personality of the victim. My observations concern the look of things. This is where the art of design begins.

Here is a one-story wooden structure with a simple hipped roof, the facade restyled with asbestos siding. Over there ashlar limestone forms a high foundation supporting walls of horizontal wood siding. Many houses feature gabled roofs, and some have porches with their own gabled roofs, a feature marking descendants of the Greek Revival. In the Midwest and plains, the style is reflected in a more common form, on the porches and rooflines. Nearly all the houses feature wrought iron, brick, or wood columns and pilasters that outline porches enclosed, screened, split by the entry door, or wrapped around one side.

What makes these taken-for-granted, seemingly obscure home features particularly interesting is that they bring to light cultural moments. My *Field Guide to American Houses* reveals how the

Greek Revival movement was influenced by such disparate events as archeological discoveries, sympathies for Greece's involvement in a war for independence, and distaste for British influence in America during the War of 1812. If an aesthetic context is a representation of sociopolitical climates, it might also serve to create an identity with that context. At the turn of the century, the garden city movement sought relief from the ravages of dirty, smelly, industrial towns by advocating living in communities planned with lakes, greenbelts, and clean buildings. The Greek Revival and its descendant, beaux arts, promoted the mystique of the grand and distinguished. The social hygiene movement I talked about in chapter 4 aimed at liberating the lower class from its atavistic impulses. Movements in architecture and design aspired to similar ends but also encouraged appreciation for culture and, according to the planning scholar Wendy Sarkissian and her colleagues, attempted to correct all the problems of the city: crime, poverty, disease, social unrest, and the segregation of races and classes.

I argued in chapters 2 and 3 how contemporary movements designed to improve quality of life and reduce crime, such as community policing, have their detractors because such movements often appear as one influential group of society trying to control and coerce another seemingly threatening group. The movements around the turn of the twentieth century were no different. Backers of the social hygiene and garden city movements lived a decidedly New England and aristocratic lifestyle. Lawrence Friedman, a Stanford University law scholar, tells us that because of a high divorce rate, expanding industrial markets, demographic changes, and a host of other structural factors, "The last third of the 19th century was . . . an era of national panic over morality, eugenics, the purity of the bloodline and the future of old-fashioned white America."

Another movement was afoot at the turn of the century to resist actively this morality-driven, class-based image for America, especially since the well-intentioned efforts of a panicky elite caused as much harm as they did good. Among the harms was the forced sterilization of those whose offspring might spread social decay, including criminals, mental patients, the handicapped, the mentally retarded, and epileptics. The resistance bore fruit in religion, jour-

nalism, art, sociology, and architecture. The Chicago-school architect Louis H. Sullivan made a conscious desire to adapt buildings to
culture, believing that since America was supposed to represent the
great democratic, classless society, then buildings should demonstrate that vision, not the excessive ornamentation and elaborately
detailed fenestration characteristic of the beaux arts, born from
class-oriented European cultures. "Buildings are outward manifestations of internal values," Sullivan said. When Sullivan set out to
build a new Farmer's and Merchant Union Bank in Columbus, Wisconsin, the Chicago Historical Society recorded his concern that
"the original bank provided no sense of its commitment to the community."

In *The Hudsucker Proxy* the joke is that the hula hoop makes
people feel a part of something—a crazy consumer fetish—but also
places a physical barrier around them. Design strategies aimed at
emancipating humans from lower-class lifestyles, in the case of the
garden city movement, or confronting elite visions, in the case of
Sullivan's style, may inject a cultural moment with some new symbols but can also lead to less welcome consequences. Sullivan's
maxim, "Form follows function," has been equated with the cold,
sterile high-rise of industrial humankind. James Howard Kunstler's
Geography of Nowhere, a tome on the disconnected scale American
building represents, cautions us that "Sullivan had a blind spot for
civic art and the public realm. [To him] only individual buildings
mattered." Although one can slight Sullivan's failure to appreciate
the complexity with which we are connected or not connected to one
another in all facets of life, it hardly seems a fatal flaw, given the
evidence that suggests, as Kunstler points out, that we still do not
build cities with an appreciation for the importance that connected-
ness plays in creating interdependency.

I am struck by the similarity between the inability of community
policing to empower citizens and to connect them to an optimistic,
democratic problem-solving orgy and Sullivan's unrealized view that
buildings have an important role to play in helping humans achieve
a progressive place in history. Not only did Sullivan not realize that
vision, but Kunstler believes Sullivan's legacy led to an architectural
style in which the car took precedence and further disconnected us

from one another. Yet Sullivan's public papers record a man infinitely more concerned with the human condition than his industrial office building model seems to convey.

In my examination of community policing for the journal *Policing,* I explain that police leaders and optimistic academicians have a history of advocating and pursuing democratic reforms and citizen empowerment, yet those efforts often come up short. Worse, reforms toward participatory styles in policing often decrease the power citizens might otherwise hold or redirect that power toward police action to the exclusion of other pressing concerns. This is so, in part, because community policing in practice is rarely articulated as a tool to forge connections as a form of social control. Instead it is articulated as a tool to forge connections to aid the police in fighting crime, or to increase the stake police have in a community by helping build citizen trust and respect for officers.

Recall the residents in that Portland neighborhood who met at a local neighborhood crime-prevention meeting, excited and ready to tackle a range of issues, including tenants' rights problems. These were problems that the residents had defined organically but that did not meet the crime-fighting agenda as conceptualized by the police. Who is to say, however, what might have happened if tenants' grievances had been part of the agenda? The residents might have developed resourceful ties with others in their neighborhoods, developed respect for the crime-prevention professionals, and set out toward strengthening an informal social control born of "collective efficacy."

Another Sullivan legacy was Herbert Gans's idea of "taste cultures" as the ultimate response to class conflict. Who are we to tell the lower classes how to express themselves? Much as my friend the public defender said on the South Fork of the American River, the great democratic experiment means a celebration for the great chain of diversity in our land. Under the theoretical rubric known as postmodernism, a great paradox followed from an academic enterprise intended to value the diverse democratic mix. It actually disconnected buildings from their relation with the whole community, and hence disconnected community members from each other, producing what Kunstler calls scary places and scary people. In keeping with this approach, our democracy must constantly cheapen itself with never-ending efforts to control scary people and places with reactionary and oppressive strategies. A tourist guide I recently met advised that totalitarian regimes are always the safest places to visit. It is high irony that Sullivan said, "In our democratic land, ideas, thoughts, are weirdly, indeed destructively undemocratic," and then went on to seed a culture that produced fear and alienation that in turn spurred controlling, undemocratic institutions and legislation. It is not incomprehensible that this should happen, just as it is not inconceivable that efforts to democratize policing should lead to more expansive police powers.

Jane Jacobs, who spent more than three decades writing about city planning and design and their relation to social problems, answers the inability of city design to deliver on its promises adequately by calling it a "pseudoscience" that has "not yet broken with specious comfort of wishes, familiar superstitions, oversimplifications, and symbols." Jacobs made this comment in 1961. Since, then, design strategies have come a long way and research on design has been abundant and methodologically sound. Still, in the next section I outline how design strategies to reduce crime continue to create uncomfortable tensions in our democracy. My argument for an alternative view of crime control and community building stems from a belief that the view we currently hold touches only on the margins of what science can offer us. Changing that view will require, in part, a change in culture and in the way we conceptualize crime fighting and problem solving. Changing that view will require an understanding about how connections, more than symbols, influence our behavior. Place-oriented crime-control strategies that do anything less are strategies that run the risk of continuing the paradox of place.

THE LEGACY OF THE AESTHETIC IN CRIME CONTROL

The aesthetic movement as it relates to architecture and urban planning became popularized as a crime-control technique around 1961 with Jacob's *The Death and Life of Great American Cities*. Harking back to Shaw and McKay's work in Chicago neighborhoods, Jacobs felt that places vulnerable to crime were not vulnerable because they harbored a criminal class; the places themselves were criminal. Their spaces had to function as a safe environment but failed to do so. Poorly designed urban and suburban landscapes placed children away from the watchful eyes of adults. Negligent window design meant fewer eyes on the street to watch people. Design placed people apart rather than helping them mix, rub elbows, and get to know one another.

In 1972 Oscar Newman published *Defensible Space*. Such space was an area designed to create a certain territorial imperative in the user. As Newman more recently said, "When common spaces associated with high-rise housing—such as community rooms and outdoor grounds—lack clear owners or are open to too many users, residents cannot assert responsibility for their safety and maintenance, and these places are left vulnerable to crime and vandalism." Like a lily pad–covered lake, which creates certain associations in the mind of a visitor on a humid summer's day, a place properly conceived and designed can create associations that convey ownership to residents or users, which in turn provides those users with a stake in protecting that area.

Finally, with Wilson and Kelling's "broken windows" thesis emerging in the 1980s, a convincing body of literature existed that demonstrated the importance of place-based crime control strategies. This body of knowledge became widely recognized and appreciated by a following that included planners, architects, government officials, scholars, and police officers. The legacy of this knowledge has resulted in three main strategies for crime fighting—Crime Prevention through Environmental Design (CPTED), target hardening, and code enforcement—civil actions designed to maintain public order and to reduce signs of decay. These strategies are similar in their placement within a cultural paradigm that honors the aesthetic and in their attempt to draw on social capital in communities by stimulating intervention-minded behavior or limiting deviant behavior, but they are distinct in their manifestation and consequence.

Crime Prevention through Environmental Design

Newman's work found a receptive audience in the United States Department of Housing and Urban Development (HUD). Frustrated with crime-plagued public housing projects, HUD now focuses considerable attention on taking what designers call unassigned space and using design elements such as varying walkway materials, fence heights, landscaping, and paint tones to achieve residents' sense of ownership and increased guardianship. According to HUD reports, one successful case involved modifying a row-house public housing project in the South Bronx in New York City. Design strategies included the use of fencing and curbs to reassign open grounds to individual residents, as well as new paths, lighting, and play equipment to improve the appearance of the project. HUD reports that the overall crime rate dropped 54 percent in the first year after these changes were made.

A second case HUD trumpets involved the reorganization of an urban residential street grid to create minineighborhoods in downtown Dayton, Ohio: "The Dayton experience showed that communities must do more than close streets—a high level of citizen participation is critical at every stage." The caveat voiced by HUD speaks volumes to the shortcomings of deterministic design strategies. They often ultimately require users to view space as a potentially scary realm requiring constant surveillance. In practice they can lead to segregation and a "fortress mentality," paradoxically making community involvement more difficult to engender.

While I was in Phoenix, I visited a local park that serves as a national model for CPTED principles. The CPTED approach takes any number of directions in the greater Phoenix metropolitan area, from implementation to marketing. The reality-based television programs aired in the Phoenix area—*Top Cops, Real Stories of the Highway Patrol, 911, LAPD, American Justice, COPS, America's Most Wanted*—include Tempe's local *Red and Blue*. Programs run throughout the day showing how CPTED principles work and how design characteristics can lead to more "eyes on the street."

In *Red and Blue*, officers give instruction on how to envision space with guardianship in mind. As one officer said, if designers think about these issues when planning new buildings, we can determine whether we are "creating the ghettos of tomorrow or safe environments of tomorrow." The officer emphasized that the citizenry has to participate, constantly make itself aware, and form a partnership. Here in the program, a playground was surrounded by a grass moat with clear borders, designed to make "abnormal users" easy to identify.

During my stay in Phoenix, Alcohol, Tobacco and Firearms (ATF) agents arrested three members of the Viper Militia for stockpiling weapons and explosives in their homes. One neighbor who lived near the house said she never saw anything out of the ordinary there. She recalled seeing people wearing sidearms and dressed in battle fatigues on numerous occasions but said that such scenes were fairly standard for her neighborhood. I wondered what it took to earn "abnormal user" distinction in crossing the grass moat surrounding that playground near Phoenix. Though he never intended this result, Newman has had to face the uncomfortable realization that "abnormal users" sometimes describes people a democracy may need to accommodate: the homeless, low-income people, groups of teens, and racial minorities. An HUD report updating Newman's concept has confessed that, "Defensible Space has been misinterpreted, and occasionally even misused, to justify design features that have merely fenced public housing or low-income residents in or out of particular areas."

Cheryl Steele, the nationally recognized community leader in Spokane, has grappled with the apparent incongruities in CPTED and with ways to establish the positive associations between residents that she sees as the key to crime control. She wonders who came up with CPTED principles and whether, in designing the model, they understood the tenuous nature of community cohesion. The focus, she says, should remain on creating a culture that encourages involvement from all community entities and on allowing that culture to permeate the rest of city services.

The beat goes on. In British Columbia, the Royal Canadian Mounted Police approve blueprints for new buildings only if they feel the blueprints have met CPTED standards. In Irvine, California, the police department sets the limit for shrubbery heights in the city parks. The police want to make sure bushes are always low enough for an officer sitting in a cruiser to see across the park. A southern California planning consultant I met outside a planned community on a gloriously bright day offered the best analysis. As a planner, he once worked for the Irvine Company and now advises companies and governments throughout the region. Although he sees the appeal of and need for CPTED principles, he also feels a profound uneasiness as planning in the public realm fast becomes the charge of traffic engineers and police departments.

Target Hardening

Marcus Felson, in *Crime and Everyday Life*, tells us that 90 percent of crime is property crime, and he identifies how the routine activities of people all too often bring potential offenders in contact with potential targets. Whereas Newman-type control strategies attempt to produce more protective guardianship in assigned spaces, the goal of routine-activity place-oriented strategies has been to limit a target's accessibility to violation. Felson argues that increases in burglary and theft rates have more to do with the steady increase of small mobile electronic appliances in our lives than with a population explosion of the criminally inclined. Laptop computers, CD players, cellular phones, and small televisions are pricey and easy to transport, hence attractive to thieves. They are also items that did not exist twenty years ago.

Although target hardening is another strategy that can lead to the "fortress mentality" and segregation of lives, very tangible rewards exist for cities and businesses investing in these crime-reduction principles. Salem Boys Automotive Repair outside Phoenix reduced a ten-thousand-dollar-a-year insurance payment to less than five thousand dollars by installing electric gates, better lighting, alarm systems, tinted and breakproof glass, and a ten-foot wall topped with razor wire around the business perimeter, and by limiting public access to the lobby and bays.

Felson admits that in glorifying informal social control through various place strategies, some elements of our community suffer: people with handicaps, the elderly, the unhealthy, and ethnic and class groups. They are all victims in a world that too readily rewards fortressing without considering other ways to achieve the same results.

Code Enforcement

A few years ago in a southeast Portland neighborhood, residents became concerned when a constant stream of visitors began coming and going at one neighborhood home. The home was owned by an elderly resident who was no longer able to maintain the appearance of her property. Her son, a known drug user, was now living with her, and neighbors believed he was using his mother's residence as a base for drug sales.

Fearing that the use of the house would encourage the spread of illegal activity in their neighborhood, the residents mobilized a community meeting. Attendees included the elderly resident, two representatives from the Portland Police Bureau, a neighborhood crime-prevention specialist, and seventeen neighbors. They discussed their concerns. At the end of the evening, the police bureau produced a contract that included all the involved parties in a "partnership" whose major goal was to "eliminate disruptive and nuisance activity and the perception of disruptive and nuisance activity" from the elderly neighbor's residence. Each party signed the contract. The police bureau agreed to "review a list of regular visitors" to the residence periodically. The crime-prevention specialist's group agreed to provide Neighborhood Watch training in the neighborhood and, among other things, to "become a repository for neighborhood complaints." The elderly resident agreed to keep her property free from illegal activity, to "allow frequent, friendly visits by the Portland Police Bureau to her house," and to extend an invitation to neighbors to visit her home. Her fellow residents agreed to keep all neighborhood property free from illegal activity, to visit the elderly resident and communicate their concerns, and to conduct Neighborhood Watch meetings.

This unique contract reflects community-based anticrime activity to identify problem locations for intervention. The process usually requires a visit by a city code officer who threatens to close the property for health and safety code violations if the owner does not improve the condition of the property or tenants' activities there. The Portland contract offers a potentially promising outgrowth of the "broken windows" model. On its surface the contract is an exciting device, because it can encourage community residents to come together to deal with a problem in their neighborhood. It is a welcome relief for a neighborhood frustrated by ongoing illegal activity. Moreover, the contract signed in Portland did not require the police to arrest anyone. As I shall explain, however, place-oriented strategies do not always approach illegal or nuisance activity with the same care exhibited in Portland.

The Portland contract is as disturbing as it is promising, for four reasons. First, the police agreed to review a list of visitors to the residence. Did the visitors know their names were being provided to the police? Aside from this civil liberty issue, the police also did not agree to do anything more than what they normally do. For instance, they failed to offer to find resources for the elderly resident that would help her maintain her property or get drug counseling for her son.

Second, the elderly resident agreed to allow police frequent "visits" to her home, a strategy that focuses on intrusive policing as the only viable tool for solving potential criminal issues. Third, her neighbors agreed to keep tabs on her residence, but there was not an explicit agreement to help her maintain her property should it fall into deeper decay, or perhaps to help her son find more constructive, legal activities to pursue. These ambitions would have gone beyond current conceptions of what constitutes crime fighting. The contract was a sad ending, really, considering that stable, vibrant communities—not surprise visits by neighbors or surveillance of our visitors—are the best assurance against illegal activity.

Finally, the son was left out of the entire process. Perhaps he did not want to attend the meeting; perhaps he felt alienated. The neighborhood decided to address its primary source of conflict through an end run by ultimately threatening his innocent mother with the loss of her property in civil proceedings should she fail to comply with their demands.

The Portland contract serves as a reminder that if cities are not clear about the specific means needed to achieve community cohesion, they can cross that thin line separating a nurturing, supportive community able to absorb and reduce deviant activity, from one that functions by increased police activity, spying, and coercion. The optimistic message conveyed by place-oriented principles is that communities play a vital role in the crime-control process. But the means offered to those communities often become confused with other strategies or redirected from their original purpose.

I return again to Santa Ana's case to demonstrate this last point. When I heard Lieutenant Bill Tegler market, in a presentation, his success in closing nuisance apartment houses in the city as part of aggressive health and building code enforcement, he went on to make the link with the "broken windows" idea. He described the famous experiment conducted in 1969 by the Stanford psychologist Philip Zimbardo upon which the broken-windows thesis is based. (Zimbardo is probably best known for his famous mock-prison experiment, in which he randomly assigned students to act in the place of a guard or a prisoner in a staged prison in the basement of a university psychology building. Zimbardo discontinued the experiment after six days when he became concerned with the brutal behavior displayed by the students assigned as guards). Tegler said that Zimbardo abandoned a car in New York City and smashed out the car window. Vandals approached the vehicle within minutes and began stripping the vehicle bare. That was the end of his Zimbardo synopsis.

Tegler got one thing right from Wilson and Kelling's thesis: signs of decay leave the impression that no one cares for a property, and hence those who are disposed to break things will pick a place where cues tell them no one cares. But I was otherwise disturbed by how Tegler managed to butcher Zimbardo's experiment. As a former student of one of Zimbardo's colleagues, I knew the experiment well, and I knew that Tegler did not come close to illustrating the fundamental finding of the experiment. I explained that the fundamental finding revealed how vandalism could occur anywhere with the right amount of "releaser cues." To test this hypothesis, Zimbardo and his colleague Scott Fraser not only left a car in the Bronx of New York City; they also abandoned one on the Stanford University campus in Palo Alto, California, a well-to-do city not known for scary urban streets. To provide cues, the license plates were pulled off both cars and their hoods were left open. According to Zimbardo, within ten minutes people began stripping the Bronx car bare. The first group was a family: father, mother, and eight-year-old son. The vandalism occurred mostly during the day, under the watchful eyes of passersby, "who occasionally stopped to chat with the looters." Contrary to popular images about who engages in vandalism, Zimbardo noted that "the adults were all well-dressed, clean-cut whites who would under other circumstances be mistaken for mature, responsible citizens demanding more law and order." Eventually children used the Bronx car as a playhouse.

The car at Stanford was left untouched for a week. Did this mean people at Stanford were more virtuous? According to Zimbardo it just meant that the Stanford environment did not contain the compounding and necessary cues that abound in a large, dirty, dense urban environment. To promote vandalism, Zimbardo and two graduate students smashed the car with a sledge hammer and watched to see if others would follow their lead. He reported an initial reluctance that was soon overcome because "it feels so good after the first smack that the next one comes more easily, with more force, and feels even better." Even after the car was thoroughly pulverized and flipped upside down, according to Zimbardo, "at 12:30 A.M. three young men with pipes and bars began pounding away at the carcass."

When I discussed Tegler's version of the experiment with others who were at his presentation, they remarked that they had thought Tegler was talking about young gang members and other street villains when he said "vandals." Tegler provides a good, though troubling, case study on how police departments fail to grasp fully the broken-windows thesis. Because Santa Ana's strategies and Tegler's marketing of them continue to gain audiences from police departments around the country and the world, the same botched analysis gets perpetuated. The Santa Ana police strategy becomes a method to "crack down" on code violators. Responding to the massive enforcement strategies employed by New York City police and concerned with the misconception about "broken windows" in theory and practice, George Kelling told *Time* magazine that there is no room in "broken windows" for "sweeps and crackdowns." At first glance these strategies seem promising, but they can lead to ill will in the community and can develop a siege mentality in the police force that will likely lead to brutality.

Like community policing, place-oriented strategies have yet to provide a way to bring disparate people back together, to help the drug addict face a problem, or to encourage a gangster to become involved in another activity. If a property owner finds he or she is renting to drug users, one Safe Streets program manual advises, "We recommend, under these circumstances, eviction." It then goes on to describe the four types of evictions allowable under the law. Not far from that mean neighborhood in the heartland where my friend Bill intervened, a city police officer praises the efforts of local code enforcement officers to close down an apartment building frequented by drug dealers and prostitutes, saying, "Now finally we can get rid of those people." Presumably some other community can have them, since the prisons and courts seem full at the moment.

≈ o ≈

As I mentioned in the previous chapter, communities are well advised to recognize that there is a definite link between signs of disorder and subsequent incivilities. Unfortunately, nowhere in my travels did those strategies in practice focus too much on those signs on the surface. George Kelling and Catherine M. Coles's 1996 work extolling the virtues of order-maintenance policing, *Fixing Broken Windows,* provides an overly optimistic glimpse of the popularity of place-based order-control strategies. They voice a passing concern for violation of individual liberties while praising community as an important variable worthy of protecting. The community is indeed the most important tool in establishing prosocial action. But it is one thing to use surface physical measures to control deviant behavior; it is quite another to use those same measures to encourage interdependent behavior and to confront the problems that bother us.

When the United States Department of Justice published a handbook that reviewed the current state of knowledge with respect to environmental crime-control strategies, the authors concluded that "no study has been able to associate physical changes with behavioral change in a definite manner." On the tree-lined streets of Bill's neighborhood, the homes all have porches and their yards are kept tidy. There are no signs of disorder; any hint of an urban jungle is nonexistent. Absent some as-yet-unknown theoretical linkage between elements in space and behavior, along with the knowledge of how that behavior can be directed toward prosocial action, I am left with the uneasy realization that community members are often reluctant participants in matters where they must police one another and that the police are all too eager to expand their influence. If the southern California urban planning consultant mentioned earlier is concerned with increasing police influence in our public realms, I would caution him that through code enforcement, target hardening, and crime prevention through environmental design, the police will have an even greater say in our private realms.

"Attendant determinism of architects caught up in their own myths" is a problem, Edward Soja tells us in his critique of spatial life in southern California, because it is "space, more than time, that now hides consequences from us, [because] these new spaces are what now push us away from the centers of power, and [because] this peripheralization is played out at many spatial scales." For Soja, spatial life is inherently political. A crime-control strategy that fails to appreciate fully the political nature of space will only perpetuate existing power imbalances. It will play the community for the hapless fool. Unless we can increase our social capital and community fortunes with our own hula hoop vision, the joke is on us, and the story we will know is the one in which the community becomes the sucker proxy.

6. New Urbanism

Connecting ecology to form community

At the ground level almost anything goes. Builders try
to outshine each other rather than fit in: "This is
America; we can do what we want."
    —A southern California planning consultant

D

o you know that in San Luis Obispo [California] the city
passed an ordinance which requires new homes to have
front porches?" Cheryl Steele asks. "It's supposed to
improve neighboring." She has just introduced me to a currently
popular theory in urban planning referred to as New Urbanism, also
known as neotraditionalism, urban and neighborhood villages, compact cities, pedestrian pockets, and residential mixing. These are
planning initiatives aimed to make builders responsible for fostering
active, mixed-use developments that are now typically missing from
the suburban landscape. Steele is a convert, having recently attended
a presentation by builders and planners who painted an inspiring
vision for Spokane based on mixed-use, high-density zoning, downtown redevelopment, and an environment scaled to human traffic,
not cars. Steele sees a way to reestablish the community that she
knows will provide the best protection against crime: "We've got to
get developers to plan communities with a mix of classes and no
gated communities. Then class A has to take responsibility for class
B. We have to encourage people to mix again, downtown."

Back in 1961, Jane Jacobs hailed Spokane's Davenport Hotel as
a "distinctive and beloved landmark . . . a major center of city public
life and assembly." Years later the hotel sat neglected, a symbol of
what the abandoned, soulless downtown had become. Today, a

Hong Kong developer has slated the Davenport for a major restoration. The developer and the city at first squared off, because the city tried to renege on a deal to provide a parking garage, but the restoration now seems on course. The Davenport has an unmistakable historical appeal, but will this appeal serve to focus the new downtown vision? Currently, few people gather in downtown Spokane. I was warned not to walk the streets after dusk. When I did, I found vast empty spaces filled only with a chilly, hollow wind. Here and there a few of the usual suspects scuttled about—drunks, teens trying to look hard, bus station transients, and prostitutes—but for the most part the downtown was empty.

Steele believes that the people who should go downtown gather at home around the television. She hopes to encourage her neighbors across the city to abandon the television set and head downtown to gather, not around a drink, but around each other, through art, games, and even singing. Steele not only believes this vision will materialize, she has a plan to make it so: family movies, a neighborhood shuttle, gathering spaces such as courtyards. Even though the police department employs her, she feels uneasy about people coming together only to fight crime, fearing that such action will further feed a paradigm in which crime becomes the all-encompassing issue. "But," she laments, "how do you show people in gated communities that it's better, this world out here?" Steele's concern is not without merit. A builder in Orange County, California, told me he can charge at least twenty thousand dollars more on the price of a home by throwing a gate around a development.

It is one thing to say that community mitigates crime and other social ills, but quite another to suggest that a failure to develop and build places able to cultivate "collective efficacy" makes all of us at least a tiny bit culpable in fostering crime. To retreat to safe, gated suburban neighborhoods at night might be seen to give streets over to undesirable elements who will commit antisocial behaviors only when the rest of us are not there to provide a check on their behavior. Luckily our culture provides a perfect out. A popular belief in this country is that personal choice should be allowed to govern behavior. On the one hand, the ethos of personal responsibility and rugged individualism makes for good advertisement copy, absolves us of political responsibility, and may even help shape a dominant American psychic tradition that promotes competition, assertiveness, and a pull-yourself-up-by-your-bootstraps mentality. On the other hand, it is an ethos at odds with the basic tenet grounding New Urbanism, and indeed other symbolic American expressions, such as "United we stand, divided we fall," "We the people . . . in order to form a more perfect union," and "A government by the people, for the people . . ." We are a nation that respects and defers to the iconic images that a unified, strong community evokes, but as a people we seem quite unable to extend the logic by admitting that a community ultimately shapes and fosters our behavior.

NEW PROMISES, POWERLESS PLACES

New Urbanism starts with the belief that planners can construct worlds that are able to foster community, which in turn will provide the collective power and informal social control needed to address problems such as crime. However, those houses in the heartland city where teens savagely kicked and beat their neighbor all sported old, well-used porches. Good neighboring was as much a ghost there as it was in the streets of downtown Spokane. As I noted in the previous chapter, changing spatial design does not always achieve the ends architects desire. This does not necessarily mean it cannot work; it may mean only that the issue is frequently examined too superficially.

My analysis of New Urbanism brought me to a road criminologists rarely travel, but more than any other theme it began to explain how we ultimately can exploit the power residing in the community framework. New Urbanism benefits from great popularity. It pits the suburban world against the dense, revitalized city. Like inner-city shooting zones and the dizzyingly vast and disconnected suburb, New Urbanist planning presents dilemmas and obstacles, but a close look shows how it might help a community mitigate crime and increase social capital.

New Urbanist ideas such as public contact, diverse property uses, and social mixing are backed by scientific support showing that such factors sustain safety. Alexander von Hoffman boasts in the

Atlantic how "bad neighborhoods" are being transformed by community-based housing—private-market public housing providing low-cost home ownership in tidy inner-city locations. The owners, responding to their new digs, are "engaged in community life like never before." Nostalgia-laden communities such as Disney Corporation's Celebration in Orlando, Florida; Laguna West outside Sacramento, California; and the Kentlands development in Gaithersburg, Maryland (known for its garage apartments), offer homes like the ones I saw in the heartland, featuring large, sweeping front porches, garages in the back, and plenty of street-facing windows.

Many opportunities for architectural firms exist if they are willing to tailor their building to New Urbanist principles. "Affordable housing" is no longer a phrase associated with decay and poverty. Some developments feature four-hundred- to twelve-hundred-square-foot cottages along the side or rear of the lot near the main house, thus providing a place where a young family member just starting out can reside or an older grandparent might find autonomy and security.

The claims of New Urbanists extend beyond benefits derived from changes in lot use and ownership. They believe that the social mix provided by a dense, human-scaled environment will reduce prejudices. Architect and New Urbanism proponent Peter Katz told the *Seattle Weekly* that mixed use allows businesses such as Starbucks to become integral residents in a neighborhood. Places such as coffee shops, Katz argues, provide gathering sites that sell community as much as they sell retail goods. A Taos, New Mexico, architect and New Age developer suggested to the *San Francisco Chronicle,* "Recycled homes in communal 'republics' can promote metaphysical well-being."

In conjuring a more salubrious world, the New Urbanist shuns the vast, ungraspable suburban scale. Suddenly the suburb, like the inner city, has become a demonic place. But the suburb remains the environment in which most Americans now live, work, shop, and play. It is also a powerful symbol for the state of community in American lives. During my stay in southern California, MGM released 2 *days in the Valley.* Starting with its title, including the self-conscious lowercase spelling of *days,* the movie was one of the many cinematic pulp wannabes created in the wake of Quentin Tarantino's *Pulp Fiction.* 2 *days* was interesting to me not for writer-director John Herzfeld's obvious attempt at a pulp romp but because I realized that the film's setting—the sun-baked San Fernando Valley suburban sprawl—was used to help create an attitude. I found that attitude romantic in the same way that cavernous downtown city streets and alleys once were in older pictures of the film noir tradition.

If a place can have an attitude, and a self-conscious one at that, then the character of the Los Angeles Valley presents a force second to few others. Few other modern places have so influenced popular cultural history. The quintessential 1980s rock band Van Halen hailed from the Valley. From Valley girlese and Vans-wearing, swimming-in-balloon-short, skate-rat fashion, to gangsta wannabes and '80s teen flicks, including all those trite John Hughes vehicles, the Valley is a suburban sprawl that leaves an indelible mark on pop culture like so much graffiti on a Van Nuys freeway sound wall.

The Valley provides an excellent glimpse into the suburban vision and psyche, because the *Escape from LA* artists inhabiting the Valley over the hill at grandmother's house have recently begun to talk about incorporating. Why, after all, should their tax dollars serve people in that other world, the *real* LA? Once the prime model of suburbia, the Valley is also far from immune to the problems associated with life over the hill, in Los Angeles proper.

The *Los Angeles Times* reported on a Saturday gathering in 1997 that recalled the "dawn of suburbia," when in 1939 some of the Valley's first residents moved into neighborhoods in Sherman Oaks. According to the *Times,* "About 50 people attended the . . . reunion Saturday, to greet old friends and savor the nostalgia evoked by the street." Most of those in attendance lived on the neighborhood street in the "1940s and 1950s, went to the same schools, played in the same backyards, invited each other to birthday parties and, generally, enjoyed the benefits of suburban living in its heyday." As one former resident put it, "This kind of street, well, there [are] not too many of them today." Forty years ago parcels might cost as little as one thousand dollars; today the area, home to actors, is lined with mansions priced at close to one million dollars.

Luckily, Valley residents had a day to revel in the nostalgia of suburbia before dealing with more pressing concerns. In the same week, a few miles north across the Ventura Freeway in Van Nuys, hearings were arranged by Sherman Oaks assemblyman Robert Hertzberg "in an effort to connect with those affected directly by juvenile crime." Further north, just across the I-5 freeway on another weekend, residents in Pacoima gathered to hold a prayer session in a desperate attempt to do something about the spread of youth gangs.

There are still other sites that suggest that although the dense, mixed-use city has lost its place in America, the suburb is born of reaction and offers little solace. Let me continue, this time down the road to the south. In the southern basin, Orange County gated communities spread across the landscape like herds of molting turtles looking for shelter from the dangerous elements. East to Riverside, developers marketing vast, sprawling tracts can barely keep pace with buyers' demand.

The messages these suburban sovereignties send visitors seem hopelessly mired in a wash of turbulent contradictions. We are told the good life awaits where, as one Irvine Company brochure announces, "shopping is easy . . . jobs are plentiful. . . . Growth is managed and orderly. . . . Travel is simple. And swift. Communities are tidy. . . . [There are] no abandoned buildings with broken windows or graffiti. . . . Residents spend much of their time outdoors. Community swimming pools, parks, school grounds, golf courses, and trails are convenient." We are told that here we have ample places to work and play. The weather pours sunshine year-round. When it does turn foul, even the rain is warm and stylish. The culture here is often envied, embraced, and exalted. The quality of life and safety here are reinforced by studies in popular magazines that receive extensive press. Planners the world over come to Irvine like pilgrims to Mecca, searching for the hidden key to the "perfectly planned community." The Italian architectural magazine *Lotus* devoted one hundred pages to the Irvine experiment. The Irvine Company celebrated the first twenty-five years of its experiment with a play on the inscription Caesar displayed after triumphing in the Black Sea—*veni, vidi, vici* (I came, I saw, I conquered)—by proclaiming, "They came, they saw, they bought."

Places such as Irvine are exquisitely planned and enormously popular. Still, I cannot help feeling a slight uneasiness. No, a massive, unsettling gnawing in the bottom of my stomach is more appropriate. It is these same suburban paradises, after all, that have served as a backdrop to other cultural images, like Steven Spielberg's *Poltergeist* and then *E.T.* In the latter film a disjointed single-parent household coped with the chaos created by an alien visitor and an unknowable, uncaring, faceless government, all within the bounds of a perfect planned community. According to the *Florida Times-Union*, film producer Edward S. Feldman thought he would have to construct a multimillion dollar set to capture that almost fake look of the idyllic, nostalgic, yet oppressive little town Seahaven for the movie *The Truman Show*. Then the producer came across the real town of Seaside, Florida, complete with narrow, brick-paved streets, unsoiled sidewalks, and charming homes. As one of the characters proclaims in the opening sequence of the movie, "Nothing you see on this show is fake. It's merely controlled."

If pop culture has caught this apparent paradox of the suburbs well, scholars have brought equally impressive analysis to bear on it. The hidden costs to the people of the LA region, blurred behind layers of ultrasunblock SPF 45, include economic, psychological, health, and political disorders.

The time I spent in southern California suburbs was time spent always getting lost. It was a strange experience that made me feel provincial until I learned that other newcomers I met were feeling the same thing. Long, wide boulevards and parkways stretched before me and around me, but my usual tools to map a city were not there: the house on the corner, the store down the street, the park next to the apartment building. Everything had become a blip on my radar as I drove past a mall set back from the street and past rows and rows of homes discretely hidden away from the parkways.

It is a little after six o'clock, on one of those beautiful late spring evenings that sometimes make southern California irresistible. I have returned to visit Irvine's Heritage Park, the pride of the fleet in city parks. After settling on my choice of parking in an obscenely large lot framing the park, I encounter a rolling, grassy plain where I count three or four soccer fields, tennis courts, a softball and base-ball diamond, a volleyball court, basketball courts with perfect nets and padded posts, multiple kiddie playgrounds, and a center lake containing ducks, geese, and a gushing fountain. On the shore near a community center, I sit in a gazebo and watch people throughout the park. Some jog on wide, clean pathways lined with sparkling trash cans, recycling bins, barbecue pits, and picnic tables. I cannot detect a single sign of graffiti or carelessly placed trash. Others play soccer, run the basketball court, huddle for touch football, or breeze across a field chasing a Frisbee. When I visited the park earlier in the day, it was empty except for one soul reading a book in the middle of a vast lawn and a Latina woman pushing two Anglo children in a stroller. Now I count about 250 people. All the groups are efficiently buff-ered from each other by large, empty, embarrassing space. And I feel as isolated and alone as I felt earlier in the day. I do not feel that I play any part in this social gathering. If by chance I wanted to sit close to a group to remind myself of my humanity, my approach would require me to cover enough ground and seem so obvious that I am sure someone might take me as a molester, kidnapper, or other sort of undesirable.

In contrast, a week before I sat in another lake-oriented park, directly adjacent to a small village called Montclair in North Oak-land, California. The village's narrow streets are usually packed all day and into the evening with people shopping, strolling from work to grab a bite to eat, and coming and going from their houses and apartments. Montclair is an old-fashioned mixed-use island. The park is equally active all day long. People walk on their lunch hour, gather at picnic tables to eat outside, or play a game of tennis. In that park, indeed in the whole village, wherever I went I negotiated around people. I bumped into them, asked permission to sit on a crowded bench, and could not help overhearing conversations. Sometimes people spontaneously created group conversation when someone smiled or laughed at a funny-looking dog or a cute baby and then another person validated the first person's gesture. The scale was small enough that close contact was virtually guaranteed.

Never once did I need my car to go shoot some hoops, shop at the drugstore, or buy lunch. The Irvine experience left me feeling empty and alone; the Montclair experience, vibrant and human.

It is the last point that most contemporary critics of the LA region experience emphasize. Mike Davis did so by decrying the demise of "heteroglossia," of the socially mixed democratic city. Edward Soja did so by noting a pathologically internalized belief in suburbia by its worshipers. Manuel Castells did so by explaining how the NIMBY (not in my backyard) syndrome—honed and perfected in places such as the Valley and Orange County's "edge cities" (to use Joel Garreau's term)—allows people to "withdraw into miniature paradises . . . or withdraw through defensive community struggles, the [NIMBY] movements, but they have not grasped the real problems and scale, the loss of power to control flow of information through space."

This is the important part: Crime is virtually unheard of in places such as Irvine and Mukilteo, but the fear of crime remains high. We try to manufacture the security and power we seek, but they are only a manufactured toy, not the networked, interdependent community we need. So tenuous is our place in this lost highway that Castells uses Tom Wolfe's *Bonfire of the Vanities* as the perfect contemporary metaphor for the fear produced by losing our grip on this controlled space: "If you get out of your particular path and your particular flow, everything can happen to you. It happens to you because everything outside the flow is uncontrolled space that is not integrated into the social experience and the social meaning of society. . . . We turn ever deeper inward, in protected hotels, protected airports, and protected business meeting rooms, all connected through telecommunications."

The fear is not felt just by suburbanites who must drive or walk in the city. As a commentary in the *Economist* observes, "Just as white suburbanites swap horror stories about ending up in the ghetto, so research among blacks in Chicago's South Side reveals widespread fears of harassment by the police or local residents should they find themselves in the suburbs after dark." I wonder whether the fear is simply a proxy for the loss of control and power we all face by losing contact with our networks in a rapidly changing world. Whatever the reasons for this defensive withdrawal, the LA suburban region is but one place that conveys to its inhabitants a reaction that comes across as exclusionary, segregated, and enclaved. In 1976 the planning firm Gruen Associates warned about the impending enclaving in southern California. The firm also noted the problems enclaving would bring, such as increased segregation and the subsequent precipitation of crime.

NEW URBANISM AND SUBURBS IN PERSPECTIVE

In all fairness, New Urbanism is not without its detractors and its potential problems. Calvin Woodward, reporting on New Urbanist developments for the Associated Press, observes that, just as in the suburbs, "each step toward self-sufficiency risks increased isolation" from the rest of the world. He also notes that "as in many new developments residents are subjected to rules galore—not like the old days." Basketball nets mounted in driveways or portable ones erected on the street remain the most debated private space issue.

A commentary in the *Economist* observes that "unless there are government policies requiring affordable housing throughout entire regions . . . New Urbanism in the suburbs will be predominantly for middle- and upper-income people." The suburbs still provide relatively inexpensive home ownership and lower tax obligations. The reality, according to the *Economist,* is that most people live in the suburbs. Many also work there. "Such people now experience the cities much as a tourist might. . . . They watch television newspictures of murder, and now riot, in the cities; they visit them occasionally; they watch films about them. And they don't like what they see and hear."

Without question America is facing a decline in the public space needed to provide a vibrant democratic mix and debate. But relying on truly public space to generate community social capital also means having to face the consequences of our current sociopolitical structure. If a sense of community is fostered, whose sense is it? What community is it? A Berkeley, California, coffee shop was creating a gathering place, as Peter Katz told us earlier. An unintended consequence resulted after the business put a bench in the front to attract chatty, coffee-buying neighbors: it attracted *all* the neighbors.

The management later decided to remove the bench because it was attracting too many bothersome, smelly, homeless individuals. Unless we are willing to contend with such uncomfortable interactions, the suburban enclave provides a ready escape.

Economically, New Urbanist strategies to revitalize cities seem problematic. According to Peter Gordon and Harry Richardson, both professors of planning and economics in the School of Urban Planning and Development and the Department of Economics at the University of Southern California, "The compact settlement projects may have a boutique appeal," but New Urbanism chiefly serves "rent-seeking downtown interests." Suburbs require fewer transportation subsidies than downtowns: "On a per-passenger-mile basis, city transit subsidies are as much as 54 times greater than auto subsidies." Suburbs still provide less expensive housing than New Urbanist developments, and furthermore, "despite expensive revitalization, downtowns compete poorly as public gathering spaces against suburban malls and 'invented streets,' such as MCA's $100 million City Walk at Universal City in Los Angeles, where the street performers do not panhandle and where the graffiti is public art commissioned by architects."

Gordon and Richardson's critique raises some real-world concerns for projects that often appeal to utopian-minded fantasies. I realize this after I leave Heritage Park and drive to Berkeley, where I attend a slide show and talk by Richard Register, on his efforts to transform the downtown into an "Ecocity" complex. For the first time I become cynical, seeing the New Urbanist movement as a naive utopian myth. Register, a former peace activist, off-and-on carpenter, and full-time Ecocity advocate, envisions a "Heart of the City Project" where the car has become the outcast and people the integral component. He wants the city to zone the area for a terraced maze of garden apartments, cafés, and commercial office and retail space, all framing a large public gathering place bounded by the restored Strawberry Canyon Creek. The creek is now contained by storm drains, culverts, and pipes under layers of asphalt.

Register was one of the forces behind Berkeley's Milvia Slow Street, a project that took a once straight, fast, and pedestrian-unfriendly street and made it zigzag, dotted it with speed bumps, and framed it with planter boxes. He also advocated for the now common curbside stencils to mark underground creeks as a reminder about where waste goes when dumped in drains. In addition, at every opportunity Register "depaves" property.

Tonight, at his talk, Register shows the eclectic Berkeley crowd a slide taken on the street fronting his organization's cooperative demonstration house. In the slide he and confederates sling pickaxes to depave sidewalk space to make way for fruit trees. He tells us the city balked at the fruit tree idea because fallen fruit can cause mishaps and rambunctious teens like to throw fruit at neighbors' houses, cars, and walkways. Register says the cooperative put a sign on the tree inviting neighbors to take a "fare share." As for the fruit-as-projectile worry, Register used a tactic that brings to mind Trojanowicz's cops in that park in Flint, Michigan: "We just talked to the neighborhood kids and we've never had any problems." He also encourages planting fruit trees in urban schoolyards so inner-city youths can get a very simple but "vivid sense for humans' connection to life," to a world that feeds us and sustains us as long as life is respected and nourished.

My cynicism with Register's hopeful plan arises as I look at his drawings for the development. I see no signage and absolutely no provision for parking. Just as well: Register wants to do away with cars. Unfortunately, as Gordon and Richardson remind us, revitalizing downtown streets by closing them off to traffic and attempting to transform them into public attractions turns city leaders into high-stakes gamblers. In some places it works brilliantly, as it did with Santa Monica's Third Street Promenade. At other sites it fails miserably. In Santa Ana, the city's efforts to create a public-courtyard feel among shops and artists' studios near Fourth Street killed the business in the two-block area that was closed to cars. In Sacramento, the K Street Promenade is one of the scariest nighttime places I have ever visited.

On a drizzly evening in Sacramento, I left an isolated, self-contained high-rise hotel to stroll the redesigned street. The city had closed K Street to vehicle traffic, repaved it with brick, dotted it with benches and planter boxes, encouraged retailers to open shops, and laid tracks for a trolley. As I strolled, I came across Guardian Angels who were patrolling after a recent robbery-homicide outside a night-club. Further on, a cop on a bicycle was writing a man a ticket for jaywalking across the brick-paved street. The closed-off corridor is supposed to feel like an open promenade, but the presence of the trolley presents a safety hazard, so the city has made it illegal to cross the street anywhere except at designated spots along its length. This ordinance restricts the free flow of foot traffic that I saw at other malls and open-air street markets.

I heard a bottle smash a block over, and a drunk stumbled from an alley. As I turned a corner heading back toward the hotel, I noticed I had picked up a follower from the shadows near a loading dock off the barren street. He was keeping pace about one block back. I closed my umbrella, tucked it under my arm, and became a different animal—wary, assertive, calculating. Under a street lamp I stopped and turned to watch him; he stopped too, still a block back. I stood there long enough to suggest to him, I hoped, that I was no tourist walking willy-nilly through the streets. He held his ground longer than I was used to in such situations. Eventually, he moved around a corner and away from me. I returned to the hotel, relaxing only when I stepped inside its marble lobby. It was segregated, it was decadent, and right then it felt good.

Projects like Register's need to draw what planners call anchors: high-interest retail businesses with big corporate-investment capital. Such businesses are reluctant to open shop in an area without, at the very least, minimal curbside parking. Corporate entities that offer developers the big anchor establishments generally prefer large, empty lots where they can establish a perimeter parking footprint or expansive malls that guarantee a huge regional draw. In designing Triangle Square, the city of Costa Mesa, California, attempted a redevelopment project similar to Register's vision. The original plan lacked housing and did not include gardens or solar greenhouses, but it did provide office space, cafés, theaters, a supermarket, and retail establishments such as Barnes and Noble, Virgin Megastore, and Niketown. The plan called for construction on three levels, all with a consistent Mediterranean style that featured stucco arches, towers, awnings, and Mexican-stone accents. From the standpoint of New Urbanists, Triangle Square's most important design feature was its "town square."

The best-laid plans of the Costa Mesa Redevelopment Agency and Triangle Square Associates met Nike. The corporation refused to take up its anchor lease unless it was ensured street-level access and the freedom to design its store facade by corporate standards, not Costa Mesa's Mediterranean style. Nike also wanted signage, and lots of it. The company turned street-side walls, originally designed as open-air market space, into blank monoliths. To meet the development's rules limiting signage, the company agreed to place nonpermanent posters of athletes on the walls. Later, without much notice, Nike carved more permanent reliefs, as it had originally wanted to do. A visitor driving southeast off the Route 55 freeway onto Newport Boulevard would see a huge postmodern dome, looking like one half of Barbarella's bra, upon which NIKE-TOWN is carved in towering, six-foot letters.

It is too easy to make the corporation entities into demons and to give up on a project before it begins. At Register's Berkeley presentation, the crowd convinces itself early during the question-and-answer period that corporate giants would make the car and retail islands prevail. Retail interests depend on the large consumer flow I described in chapter 4. Those interests can anchor a development with millions of dollars, because they know how to bring people to their locations. They have seen times when redevelopment works and when it fails, and few can risk tucking the bank away behind a garden balcony five blocks from the nearest parking. Register remains hopeful that consumer interests will change and that people will not shy away from parking their cars blocks away from where they are going. But on the mornings I spent in that crowded Montclair village in North Oakland, sitting on a bench outside Peet's Coffee and Tea, I watched hurried residents from the hills circle the block a half-dozen times trying to find a spot right in front of the coffee store. Others parked in red zones. Still others parked in the middle of the street, prompting near riots from the drivers of cars lined up behind.

New Urbanists' greatest struggle may be not with the corporate giants but with Americans who live in affluence compared to the rest of the world, who can afford a fairly autonomous existence, and who refuse to walk when they can circle the block over and over. As Gordon and Richardson note, New Urbanism is just another market taste, but the market preference remains for suburban living where home owners can purchase any needs a community might provide. "Developers are very market-conscious," they tell us. "Builders are well aware of the strong consumer preference for the single-family detached home."

I return from Berkeley to meet with a planner in southern California. I am looking at a human-made lake in Mission Viejo, California. I have been told by the planner that the lake is supposed to give identity to the community and that I am supposed to feel that identity. If elements like lakes, bridges, and parks do not actually change behavior, perhaps they are still reflected in our cognitive processes by making us feel a certain linkage with a place. I cannot say how the lake will work for others. For me it provides serenity, peace, and a refreshing break from the car. The lake offers momentary comfort, but it does not tie me to that community. Fortunately or unfortunately, I grew up (as I suspect most of us did) tied to place by my relation to those around me and by the roles I took in that connected world, not by the lakes and trees in my town. Yet the market demands lakes, streets with names like Memory Lane, and homes described in brochures as "enormous" and "palatial" but able to "radiate charm, romance, vitality."

At a presentation with planners and builders in Irvine, I am amazed to discover that the builders themselves are befuddled by the demands buyers place on them. The builders research and analyze their market well, and they are driven to build by that market, erecting the "jive-plastic colonials" that James Howard Kunstler talks about in *Geography of Nowhere*. The houses we dream about with our smaller families today, according to *Metropolitan Home*, require more interior light, expansive open spaces, and bigger rooms. Communal spaces are in demand within homes. The house as loft has become a popular theme. Twenty-foot ceilings and even twelve-foot shower walls mark this style. An Irvine Company builder puzzles how the buyer can get it all, an interior mansion feel and a large yard at a cheap price. Yet he tries to deliver. The style becomes the key, and outward symbols become the expression the owner seeks.

Builders deliver on buyers' demands with gimmicky but powerful imagery: "colonialist" interior-passage doors, "relaxed Gold Coast living." Come live here and "take your place in history," an ad for a San Juan Hills development advises. "Pamper your car and yourself," another ad says, featuring the proximity of home to a designer car wash. Buyers can retreat into a house with burglar and fire protection, where "temporary access to certain areas of the home can be controlled." Whole houses are wired for audio and video, advanced telecommunication and room monitors, and elaborate heating and ventilation that provide "system profiles" to respond to your needs even before you arrive home.

Charles Jencks, in *Heteropolis,* worries that architecture and planning are giving in to our fears, not building on our ambitions and hopes for vibrant communities. He points to the popularity of the "LA–Style" fashioned by world-renowned architect Frank Gehry. The LA–Style makes house-as-fortress a viable option. Jencks places blame for community demise squarely on the shoulders of architects and builders who have created the "rootlessness" and "spatial estrangement" that are at once trendy and aesthetic but hopelessly bound in class symbolism.

In a *Nightline* interview, Gehry described his impetus for designing buildings stylishly clad in long, whimsical metal sheets, corrugated galvanized plating, and chain-link fencing: "The world under democracy creates chaotic cities. I'm trying to resolve forces; these forces are coming at me. It's like using jujitsu. There's a guy coming at me and I redirect the energy." No one could have said it better. Modern architecture and building exist to battle a metaphoric street crime, an attacker coming out of the darkness. In describing his controversial fortress-style house, Gehry notes, "When you go in there it's serene." His fundamental drive seems noble enough. He does not want to "retreat to the nineteenth century or live with the times"; he wants to do something new, so that he can tell his grandchildren there was an alternative that allows us to go forward rather than back.

I am caught by the idea that going forward can be achieved by building upon symbols of attack and upon a desire to create safe forts where we can live like colonial powers. I am not sure I sense a need for jujitsu on a city street when I am surrounded by people I know and trust, people with whom I am connected. Going forward can also mean connecting and becoming social beings again. The New Urbanist step requires one to feel naked at first as we shed the warm interior hearth. Going forward by connecting can also mean finally seizing the benefits offered by an informal social control and social capital that no amount of money can buy and by a power we can hope to seize only symbolically in our fortress enclaves.

≈ o ≈

The appeal of New Urbanism is a story worth knowing, in part because it signifies an expansion of our often limited view of crime control, and in part because it expresses a recognition for the appeal of the cohesive, interdependent, self-contained community. As with the stories told in earlier chapters, the story of New Urbanism also presents the risk that the self-contained community will turn inward and miss that important requirement of involving disparate actors across various class and race groups.

The story of New Urbanism can become a heroic epic as it helps orient people back to place and as it builds on the power of a connected people. Or it can become a tragedy as it fuels further isolation and paves the way for private police to exclude and to partition us away from those whose behavior we fear.

In the next chapter I provide a more scientific understanding of how connecting with others provides for a powerful informal control on aberrant behavior. The story of New Urbanism we should seek to know is the story that understands how shaping place to build connections offers solutions to a number of potential ills, the least of which is that it may prove too costly for our economic and moral health to build and maintain fortresses and to hire legions of private police to guard our homes.

7. The Power of Connection

Understanding participation and ties

"I've never done a single thing I've wanted to in my
whole life! I don't know 's I've accomplished anything
except just get along."
 —Sinclair Lewis, *Babbitt*

To understand how connecting delivers a simple, eloquent, and powerful form of control and provides social benefits beyond safety, I return to Philip Zimbardo and a more detailed analysis of his 1969 work that served as the basis for the "broken windows" thesis. Few have taken the time to discern the fundamental points Zimbardo made in this work, of which the car vandalism experiment was only a tiny component. Zimbardo's piece provides an illuminating reminder that each generation is swept up by appeals for moral order and by fear that chaos is run amok. It also provides a glimpse into a historical moment in psychology that subsequently shaped cognitive science and created a healthy concern for a complete lack of community resilience but still stressed individual rights.

For the 1969 Nebraska Symposium on Motivation, Zimbardo wrote a meandering chronicle mixed with rhetoric, mythology, literature, and several field experiments. His intent was to address the then-popular scientific belief in cognitive control. Humans were said to possess "virtually limitless potential" that allowed them to gain "freedom from behavioral proscriptions imposed by [our] history, psychology, and ecology. Indeed, thinking and believing can make it so!" Zimbardo worried that while scientists were busy "myopically" uncovering this control in the laboratory, "all hell was breaking loose outside in the real world." He chronicled the era's suicides, self-mutilation, rapes, murders, mass murders—including those committed by Charles Whitman at the University of Texas and Richard Speck, who strangled and stabbed nurses—child abuse, the theft and vandalism of marauding teens, car drivers' use of weapons against one another (sound familiar?), moral decay (made evident in public nakedness, the high divorce rate, and the public showing of pornographic films), drugs, promiscuous lifestyles, and the "impulse-dominated hedonism bent on anarchy" reflected in the hippie movement.

I might stop here to argue, as others have, that deviance is a product of a society's failure to create, as Zimbardo said, "obligations, liabilities, and restrictions imposed by guilt, shame, and fear." Political scientist James Q. Wilson, for instance, has spent a career pointing to a decline in Victorian principles and an increase in freedom of expression in the 1960s as the keys to understanding America's tumultuous, violent period since that time. Former secretary of education William Bennett has written extensively on the importance of a moral culture, emphasizing, as I read him, that if a people feel displaced and confused and face violence and disorder, it is because the obligations and restrictions Zimbardo talked about no longer exist. Not only do they not exist, we make no effort to teach them to our children.

Zimbardo, however, did not stop with such examples. With anger and poignancy he also looked at police squads that, when called to evacuate student demonstrators, brutally, viciously, and unceasingly beat the students. He brought up Vietnam atrocities in which whole villages were wiped out, including women, children, and animals. He reminded readers about torture and rape at an Arkansas state prison, prostitution rings at a state psychiatric ward, the locking away of the aged in minimally adequate nursing homes to die slow deaths, and "the hypocrisy which underscores this assault on humanity [that] is seen in society's demand for revenge over one crime while ignoring a second and participating in a third."

Zimbardo's effort was not to demonstrate that the era signaled a cultural decline in morality created by television, bad parenting, or the welfare state. He did not put the cart before the horse, a crucial analytical error moralists so often seem to commit. Instead he changed the causal ordering of what he observed around him to assert that a mobile world carelessly shedding its communal and familial ties *led* to bad parenting, a dependence on welfare, and a state in which deviant cultural messages gained importance over the community's interests. In this "Deindividuation," social obligations were null and void. Social forces making personal interaction more anonymous were the culprits that likely led to social decay. In short, we were a nation of strangers. We were no longer receiving the multiple sources of feedback that would allow us to live an "individuated" existence, that is, a more prosocial one wherein morality might be mutually constructed out of common experience, not neatly packaged into a formula peddled by morality brokers. We were also strangers to ourselves. We seemed to be acquiring power, but it was expressive power; actually we were gaining individual estrangement.

The experiment with the autos in New York and on the Stanford campus demonstrated not so much that "releaser cues" were needed to overcome social prohibitions against vandalism, but rather that we could all be driven, in the right context, to exhibit antisocial behavior. Throughout the period, simple but ingenious experiments such as Zimbardo's were revealing that people could do just about anything, given the right social framework. The most chilling of these experiments was conducted by Stanley Milgram at Yale University beginning in the mid-1960s.

Milgram ran a series of experiments with individuals from diverse occupational, racial, ethnic, and class groups. A given subject was instructed by a researcher, who wore a lab coat and was said to be part of a study on learning, to deliver increasingly painful electric shocks to a second subject if that second subject answered test questions incorrectly. The study on learning was a ruse, the painful electric shocks were not real, and the test-taking subject was acting in concert with the researchers, but the subject delivering the shocks did not know this. In his final experiment, Milgram discovered that "with numbing regularity good people were seen to knuckle under the demands of authority and perform actions that were callous and severe. Men who are in everyday life responsible and decent were seduced by the trappings of authority."

Zimbardo and Milgram needed to address this dilemma: At first glance a society with strong community bonds, where people behaved and conformed, might seem like the ideal, one where the Victorian standards Wilson talked about would hold sway over everyone. At second glance this society would provide only the "delusions of social and economic security, collective political strength, and personal approval," as Zimbardo declared, and might easily lead to atrocities such as the Holocaust or the internment of Japanese Americans in the United States during World War II. Zimbardo cautioned, "Obedience requires a myth making process of authority figures and our submission to them." We can be controlled and manipulated, he warned, because we insist on believing we maintain "personal control" over situations and are insensitive to "social forces and discriminable stimuli within the situation, which are in fact the potent determinants of action."

Zimbardo's answer to this potential conflict was to argue for a world that allows for "individual uniqueness, singularity, and personal pride" and that does not increase anonymity. If Wilson mocked participatory democracy as a solution to social ills, Zimbardo would have us use participatory styles, if only to give every person a taste of his or her humanity, a voice in the great mix in which it is too easy to become lost, to become a number, another cog in the wheel: "When a dehumanized person has become an object, then it may be that the only means he can use to get anyone to take him seriously and respond to him in an individuated way is through violence."

In many ways, Zimbardo is dated and sexist by his historical moment in writing. He equated deindividuation and its resulting irrational behavior with the "female" impulse. He urged people to "resist urban planning which nurtures sterile, drab sameness and wipes out neighborhoods where people are recognized by others and are concerned about the social evaluation of others." He railed against wiping out inner-city neighborhoods to build high-rise public housing projects. Milgram also challenged city life for its density, overload, and heterogeneity that might make one more susceptible to losing close bonds with others and to succumbing to external stimuli and their dangerous consequences.

Although both scientists were right to foresee the public housing nightmare that would follow, they neglected to understand fully that deindividuated behavior is not irrational so much as it is a good strategy for its context, and that suburbs might also lead to a sameness and a drabness that could produce anxiety and fear in their residents, further separating them from the people who make up a community.

Zimbardo gives us an appreciation for situational and structural determinants, but that is not the end of the story. On the one hand, increasing opportunities to come in contact with others who are different from us may afford the best opportunity to encode positive information about their lifestyles, since we tend to associate routine activities with comfort and security. On the other hand, if we do not enjoy routine that exposes us to others, then we are left to the mercy of cultural devices—the media, myths, and politicians—that may paint an overly stereotypical picture of the world. Increasing contact with others also has an advantage in strengthening our social networks.

Charles Tilly and Peter Bearman are two sociologists who have disputed mainstream representations of power, status, mobility, and stratification and who suggest that the complex, often imperceptible chain of networks in our lives holds the key for understanding our place in the world. We do not suffer from anomie; we suffer from a breakdown of measurable and important links that provide everything from physical health benefits to economic resources.

With each passing day we are gaining more evidence on how social networks can prevent disease and mental illness, and can help us survive major market and demographic transitions. Just as individuals can become autonomous, self-contained entities, so too can communities. Although such strength and autonomy may first seem to act as a buffer against potential conflict, in an interesting reanalysis of a famous observational neighborhood study, Mark Granovetter demonstrated in 1973 how resolute community bonds that suggest self-reliance and independence can have deleterious effects.

In 1962 Herbert Gans wrote about Boston's West End as a model interdependent, self-contained community that provided controls and support for its residents. Unfortunately, the West End was unable to mobilize to thwart redevelopment forces. The community was eventually destroyed, even though Gans had found it to be a thriving, successful community. Granovetter, in reexamining the West End story, found that Gans had missed something important. Granovetter pointed out that the West Enders were extremely internally cohesive but lacked essential ties with resources outside the neighborhood and across the city. Granovetter concluded that a multitude of such outside ties (what he termed "weak-ties") proved more important for the survival of a community—especially in a case where political affiliations were significant—than strong ties within the community.

The cognitive scientist Arthur Neal tells us that social isolation and a reliance on inner resources can lead to a negative feedback loop in which one feels rejected by one's larger society. Neal suggests that this feeling of rejection may take the form of longing for a "golden age." A group, neighborhood, or community that can be looked upon as a coherent order from the standpoint of well-integrated group members may be experienced by a stranger as an extremely complex maze that fails to bind individuals together into a common moral community. Ideas like New Urbanism, for example, provide a framework to envision structures that can add permanence and durability, which is a key, according to Neal, to establishing social relations. Proponents of New Urbanism, however, must remember that linkages across community, class, and race are as important as forming strong bonds within places.

≈ o ≈

A few years ago a new highway system was needed in London, England, to alleviate traffic congestion. In designing one, planners overlooked how the new highway would relate to the larger structure and needs of the entire transportation system. As a result of this planning omission, the new road actually increased congestion in southeast England.

I like this road example, provided by the transportation specialist Jefferey Johnson, because it helps illustrate the limits of our efforts to alleviate social problems with planning, and it also helps clarify how our efforts to alleviate crime are bound by the same complex set of relationships. A roadway plan, just like a planning theory or a crime policy, can provide ways to structure an environment so that the road either facilitates smooth traffic flow or aggravates it. "Urban and metropolitan road networks are very complex systems with ambiguous boundaries," Johnson says. "Everything is connected to everything else, and atomistic approaches will inevitably result in unforeseen interactions and problems."

If flat asphalt roadways are as complex as Johnson tells us they are, then our social systems present infinitely more complexity and ambiguity. In the loss of place, in our modern movement to hold tight to our particular flow, "poetry is the last thing to be lost," Manuel Castells laments. The poet—like Louis Sullivan's architect and Richard Register's "Ecobuilder"—is in tune, sensitive to our world and to our intimate needs. Ultimately the marketer is not sensitive to our needs. Nor is the police officer, judge, code enforcement officer, builder, legislature, or journalist. Who can paint that crime scene in the heartland? How can we capture the front-porch world Cheryl Steele envisions? Who can tell us what we need to know about it, what we need to know about ourselves? Whoever and whatever "it" is, "it" will come only when we allow ourselves thinking that is bold, creative, and expansive.

"It" will come when we seek stories that tell us less about what morality and controls we need to place on one another and more about what resources, opportunities, and connections we might share as a community. If Zimbardo is right, there is a certain poetry to what his experiments suggest, a poetry so eloquently uttered generations ago by sociologist Emile Durkheim: "We are moral beings only to the extent that we are social beings," and not the other way around.

8. Communitarianism
Using laws to fashion community

I don't care what law it takes, I just want them to stop
welfare mothers from having more criminals.
—Housewife in the Pacific Northwest

Although the woman of the epigraph did not say it, she did not need to. The young mother and housewife who showed so much disdain for welfare mothers and for what she felt was their terrifying progeny was telling me that black teens scare the hell out of her. She did not come right out and say it because she probably would have thought herself a racist for doing so. Before she made her remark, she and I had been talking about crime and particularly about disturbing trends in the incarceration rates of black males. Her husband, a literate and successful man, dismissed my part of the discussion as "academic liberals finding the evidence needed to make some political statement." In frustration over any conceivable short-term or long-term solutions to her fear, the woman ended the discussion with her plea to stop the criminal breeding mills.

There are many ways to address this woman's view. I suppose I could go toe-to-toe with her logic and point out its flaws. I might show her how her view is shaped by the media and by political rhetoric. I might condemn her for having such a view and point out how destructive it is to a community project. I could do a lot of what academics regularly engage in, but I suspect I would get only as far as another dismissal by her husband that I was a liberal academic using only evidence that worked to my advantage. However, I am also struck with the "realness" of her fear. By "realness," I mean that this fear limits her freedom. She shops at malls only during the day, always drives the car with the doors locked, and refuses to travel through unfamiliar sections of her city. She watches her children like a hawk, and even in the daytime she seals herself behind dead-bolted doors and locked windows, accompanied by a large dog. All this in as safe and quiet a neighborhood as any American could hope to live in. To point out the fallacy of her logic or to insist that it emerges from the media would only invalidate her fear and place the blame on some other source. It is time to move beyond blame.

This housewife lives the life of a prisoner, and I am saddened by it. When I was in the initial stages of writing this chapter, I glimpsed more of that fear at a stoplight on a corner in Oakland, California. As I sat in my car and waited for the light to change, I noticed an elderly white woman, who looked like a frail and kindly grandmother, climb from her car and also wait for the light to change so she could cross the street.

My first reaction was to think her presence strangely out of place. The hour was late and I was not used to seeing somebody's grandmother in this section of town. She wore a long, flowing evening gown, making her appear even more unusual. I know she was aware of her vulnerability, because as the light changed she hesitated ever so slightly, and stopped advancing across the street. In a nearly imperceptible movement, as if confused, she started to veer off toward the other crosswalk and toward my car instead of ahead as she intended.

What she had seen ahead was a young black man crossing from the other direction. In the next instant she, and then I, noticed two lovers, arms wrapped casually around each other, turn a corner and fall in line behind the young black man. The grandmotherly woman then returned to her original course. I felt a tinge of sadness for her. What should have been a simple trip from parked car to front door across the street was a moment filled with queasy apprehension.

I was just as sad for the young black man, who appeared so self-conscious of the fear he generated that his attempts to look docile and unthreatening seemed to tear at his humanity. In his first few steps across the street, he looked as if he wanted to flee from the entire scene. He hesitated, then dropped his shoulders as if to resign himself to the situation. When the couple were behind him he continued on but kept his eyes focused away from the older woman. By the time he neared her in the middle of the crosswalk, he had contorted his head and shoulders so much that I felt I was in a time machine watching a subjugated and compliant black cross a street in the Jim Crow South.

I sat watching this awkwardly choreographed nightmare for so long that I missed the light. And as I sat and waited for the light to change again, a sinking feeling overtook me: even if some cities are seeing great drops in crime or our nation is experiencing a renewed belief in community, we are a long way from realizing the cohesive, nurturing, interdependent, and connected community.

If such a community could provide as good a control of crime and as strong a feeling of security as a society could want, why then is it so difficult to find or fashion such a world? Why must a young housewife irrationally fear for her safety, a grandmother cross a street so unsteadily, and a young black man risk losing his humanity?

Consider a textbook situation: city leaders dedicated to building community; police officers trained to exploit community power; citizens ready, willing, and able to walk their streets and to help one another during crises; a shared culture that values community and altruistic behavior; spatial environments designed to make people feel a part of a community; and neighborhoods and cities planned in such a fashion that they induce people to get to know one another, to rub shoulders, and to form community in all the glorious ways imaginable. So far I have examined each one of these elements and have found each fraught with difficulties. Worse still, each potential promising ingredient in the recipe to build community can paradoxically undermine community cohesion by merely preserving (at best) or amplifying (at worst) existing power imbalances as well as the racial and class divisions that exist in modern society.

As I have attempted to convey, American society is peopled by mobile and relatively autonomous citizens. Two things nearly all community building depends on are geography and people who are not in transit. Building community among rootless, transient populations or in places devoid of geographic boundaries is a poor bet. However, there is another possible ingredient that I found during my travels. In theory, this ingredient transcends geography and time. Like an omnipresent god, it is with us all the time. Indeed, our culture has come to depend on it, to exalt it, and yet to hate those who know its every nuance and can exploit it. I am speaking about law.

By law I mean specifically, as my *Webster's New Collegiate* advises, "a binding custom or practice of a community," so formally recognized as to be legislated. What changes the law, in the broadest and crudest sense, are our cultural constructions, our fears and ambitions. Thus, just as I have revealed a desire for a return to the power found in all things communal, there is an explosion in a type of legal theory that asks law to manifest that desire. The name given this explosion is communitarianism.

Philosophy professor Kelley L. Ross notes, communitarians believe that laws "communicate and symbolize those values that the community holds dear." A communitarian would argue against, for example, the repeal of drug laws, since such a move might send a message approving drug use. Ross, a critic of communitarianism, argues that the belief in the moral message that law provides "is a common response from both Conservatives and Liberals; but it is not right. The proper role of laws is to forbid judicial wrongs (of negligence, violence, and fraud) and protect judicial rights (of person, property, and contract). The law should not be used to send any 'messages.'"

Ross is unfortunately in the minority. Communitarianism is now championed as a way to institute moral guidance and to resolve numerous social problems. "The communitarian movement has come in for a good deal of attention in the last few years," according to an editorial in *First Things,* a journal of religion and public life. "It is the baby of sociologist Amitai Etzioni, and its platform is at least a movement toward the side of the angels in our political and cultural wars." Seat belt laws and motorcycle helmet laws represent quintessential communitarian legislation. As Ross tells it, under such laws, "riders have a duty to protect themselves in such a way as to not impose a burden on the public through their injuries." These laws prescribe an appealing perspective that says we should all will-ingly give up just a little liberty for the good of the community, so as to revive a new community spirit. The movement, Ross says, "pro-motes an effort to restore the notion of responsibility and establish a balance between rights and responsibilities. There has actually been talk of building a 'Statue of Responsibility' on the West Coast as the counterpart of the Statue of Liberty in New York harbor."

I should make it clear that I have touched only marginally on the topic of communitarianism. I would caution the communitarian-minded reader that for two reasons I will leave untouched a great deal of ground. First, Stanford University professor Mark Cladis, who has done the legwork and thoroughly examined as much com-munitarian legal theory as a reader could desire, observes that "an energetic and often volatile debate can be heard in many academic circles." This debate has its finger in the communitarian movement as well, which is the source, as I have briefly examined, of its own hotly contested positions.

One part of the debate (there are really two debates, but they are theoretically interrelated) "might read something like this," Cladis says. "There is an argument between those who maintain that truth and knowledge are independent of human thought . . . and those who claim that truth and knowledge are made by human thought." One consequence of this part of the debate is illustrated by a paper presented to the 1994 Citizenship and Cultural Frontiers Confer-ence at Staffordshire University, England. Community, according to the presenter, is a "contested concept," a relative term "that oper-ates on many political, cultural and spatial levels (local, civil, national, transcultural, global). . . . 'The politics of community' must thus address the question of how 'community' can coherently and noncoercively allow for the self-determination of the various 'communities' within, and hence constitutive of, its identity."

The second part of the debate goes directly to communitarian-ism and tries to wrestle with what Cladis calls a belief that "the liberal vocabulary of individual rights [is] incompatible with, and antagonistic to, the communitarian vocabulary of virtue, tradition, and community." Both parts of the debate—universality versus rela-tivism, and individual versus community—seem a bit artificial to

Cladis. He notes that the sociologist Emile Durkheim wrestled with the same issues more than a hundred years ago and concluded that there is no real conflict between the individual and the community, inasmuch as a belief in individual rights is part of the community narrative.

As for the question of universality and relativism, Cladis states that the debate really "takes on a myriad of shapes," depending on whether one is discussing literary criticism or physics. The pragmatist in me agrees with Cladis, especially since agencies such as the police do not trifle with notions like a "contested concept" of community. They are apt to apply their definition of community to devising programmatic objectives. It is essential, in recommending policy that draws on community power, then, that I work within the parameters of such definitions.

I also want to steer clear of too much theoretical discussion of legal scholarship for a second pragmatic reason. Cladis points out that scholars embroiled in various aspects of communitarian debate—among them Robert Bellah, Amy Gutman, Ronald Dworkin, Alasdair MacIntyre, John Rawls, Richard Rorty, and Michael Walzer—often do their work in the relatively detached environs of "Plato's cave." At times the debate takes on the feel of the privileged, jargon-infested, academic chest-poundings I warned about in my introduction. Rather than join this fray, I hope to use the observations I made during my travels to end this book with a workable set of suggestions for creating and drawing on community power as a crime-control technique. I anticipate that by the end of the next chapter a police chief, police officer, planner, community activist, or mayor can apply these suggestions. I also want to give credit to the theoretical ramblings; my jest about jargon is made out of respect. Such discourse is important, but it is beyond the scope of my project here.

My purpose is to come away with some pragmatic and immediately applicable view derived from the very popular communitarian framework. I will do this by returning again to the fieldwork and grounding my analysis in a case story. This story is based on an interview and visit with a minister and his family in a community church in the Pacific Northwest. It illustrates a critical element in the communitarian debate. The minister, once part of a tight-knit, conservative community, found that the law-and-order power mandated to the state to curb crime can also reach out and harm the law-abiding. From this story I hope to shed light on the usefulness of laws in fashioning community.

STRANGE BEDFELLOWS

In the 1980s, the minister, whom I will call Chuck, served a small congregation in a town overlooking the scenic Columbia River Gorge in northern Oregon. Ties among the townsfolk overlapped in many ways. With Portland only forty minutes to the west, some town members worked in the city; others were local business owners. Church members belonged to both groups. Some neighbors who were connected closely to the town during the day, by work or retirement, were able to meet once a week in the shadow of Mount Hood for potluck luncheons. Although Chuck's sponsorship brought about these luncheons, they were not held with any special agenda or religious purpose in mind. The goal was to share and visit and, more important, to welcome people from the community.

Town citizens often wore a variety of hats. Chuck was also a volunteer firefighter and the medic for the town fire department. Young people balanced their activities between the lure of Portland's and Seattle's colleges and entertainment centers and the security and nurture provided by the town. Like the adults, local youths served integral roles in the town, from helping neighbors with chores to planning and assisting in town and church events. Under Chuck's ministry, the church played an important role but a highly informal one. It offered a gathering place and a resource. Families hit by hard times could rely on town and church members to take them in, to provide employment contacts, or to supply food and clothing.

The important central role the church played in Chuck's town is not an unusual one in America. Some of the sharpest criticisms of Etzioni's manifesto on communitarianism, called *The Spirit of Community,* have come from religious circles. In particular, the editorial in *First Things* notes that although even the editors were initially supportive of communitarian thinking, that support has been undermined by a "potentially fatal weakness in the communitarian vision": They are ideals that "pay almost no attention to religion." When communitarians do discuss religion, "it is often tied to intolerant excess-religious faith and authoritarian thuggery."

"For communitarianism to ignore religion is to ignore the largest associational (i.e., communitarian) pattern in American life," the editorial in *First Things* says. "Religious differences can fragment a movement, to be sure, but a communitarianism that does not address how we should live with our deepest differences would be a pretty timorous and feeble thing." The *First Things'* warning about fragmentation is important, because some of the tension that I investigated in Spokane's east-central COP Shop was attributable to a power struggle between two neighborhood pastors. Still, like the community police officer who fails to understand that civil action is often born of a desire for political action and thus misses opportunities to mobilize citizens, communitarians must realize what the editors of *First Things* remind us: "Alexis de Tocqueville meant when he said that 'religion is the first political institution' of American democracy."

If, however, communitarians worry that religious groups will attempt to use laws to advance theological ideas, their fears are not unfounded. In a system where law is king, those who seek a voice or strive for validation often must do so through the law. I am not suggesting we neglect the role law plays in our lives. Law is important, especially considering its role in recent civil rights history. Just how important it is in fostering community or advancing each new cause célèbre is another question, however.

While the communitarian's basic agenda may aim to foster a responsive and civic-minded world, a reliance on the law becomes most troubling when coupled with the criminal justice enterprise as the problem solver of society. As each group's cause receives its fifteen minutes of law, such action seems to mean bringing penalties and punitive scope to bear on some other group of individuals.

Finding validation for stemming domestic violence means arresting and prosecuting more batterers. Achieving a voice for children's rights and safety means finding more molesters, satanic abusers, child-harmers, and deadbeat dads and bringing them to justice. Drawing attention to the slaughter on the nation's freeways each year due to drunk driving means stepping up penalties for those driving while under the influence. Trying to impress upon citizens the need for a civic culture in their neighborhoods means unleashing an army of code enforcement officers on city streets, bringing cops in to sweep away the riffraff, encouraging district attorneys to seek court injunctions against kids who are in gangs to keep them from gathering together, punishing parents who fail to raise their kids "correctly," and evicting tenants who contribute to disorder and decay.

For communitarians, social sanction is created by the law. Chuck, a relatively conservative Christian minister, at one time might have agreed with such a premise, especially given the conservative Christian movement's stand on abortion rights. Instead, Chuck now also holds that social sanction comes from a community process dependent on establishing relations and giving individuals voice, not on an overarching law. He believes this as a matter of experience, because of an event that made him realize that the absence of such a process might alienate even the most law-abiding individuals and might cause them to seek to undermine the very system of law upon which they formerly relied.

THE GORGE ACT

Chuck and his family no longer live near the Columbia River, and the community he once ministered has changed. As I make my way along the interstate toward the town, windsurfers gather in the afternoon sun on the Columbia. The river is also home to the Grand Coulee Dam, the Hanford Nuclear Reservation, and dwindling salmon reserves for Pacific fishing fleets. It provides recreation, power, food, and tourist dollars. The river thus seems a likely resource that a society might want to protect through the law.

Chuck's old town sits nestled back behind the southern gorge ridge. The road off the interstate to the town winds through a canopied rain forest lush with ferns and conifers. The weather has been unusually warm and humid lately, but the temperature along this road feels even hotter and the air suffocating. I pass a weathered, nearly empty roadside café and motel. Further along, the road leaves the forest and emerges onto a plateau facing Mount Hood, where I find Chuck's former town.

In 1986 the federal government decided to protect the steep forested ravines and canyons that lie behind Chuck's town in order to preserve the Columbia watershed. The act to create the Columbia River Gorge Scenic Area became a nightmare for Chuck and his fellow residents. What is important for my purpose here is to observe how townsfolk, many of whom were both fundamentally conservative and law-abiding, become so alienated that they formed a militia and contemplated illegal acts to cope with the government's plans.

Chuck tells me the reason for the militia movement in his town was the residents' complete loss of representation and voice. "We never felt we were a part of a process that ultimately was buying our land." Two events generated even greater animosity. First, while Chuck and his fellow residents were out of the loop, outside real estate interests were somehow in the loop, because they were buying homes lining the gorge. A nonprofit San Francisco organization bought hundreds of acres and later sold the land back to the government at inflated values. Second, a county commissioner who served Chuck's area resigned from office following a scandal involving the commissioner. Unfortunately, the seat he vacated was left empty during the remaining hearings concerning the Gorge Act. "Essentially," Chuck says, "we felt we had no representation at all during the entire Gorge Act process."

Law-abiding citizens contemplating forceful action against the government make strange bedfellows with, say, urban gang members faced with court injunctions that limit whom they may and may not associate with. Surely one cannot equate perpetrators of gang warfare with disgruntled militia wannabes in a bucolic Oregon town. What they share in common is that the sense of anarchy generated by the Gorge Act is a product of the same communitarian perspective that limits a gang member's freedom: "the greatest good for the greatest number." A district attorney might argue successfully to limit the freedom of gang members because the rest of us demand it. The law used to carry out the utilitarian perspective becomes a nondiscriminating beast and pursues the "greatest good for the greatest number" at any opportunity. Saving the Columbia watershed became an issue for urban Oregonians as well as people thousands of miles removed from the events taking place in Chuck's town.

That this situation should cause such consternation among Chuck's townsfolk is no surprise to the Stanford scholar Mark Cladis. By our limiting the freedom of gang members who might terrify us, grandmothers can walk the streets freely and the housewife at the beginning of this chapter can shop where and when she pleases. The premise provides for a flattering and hopeful solution to crime—perhaps. According to Durkheim, however, a system that relies on such a process will breed anarchy or militia movements. This is, as Cladis observes, because our "desires and reasons [are] socially spun dispositions, beliefs, and skills" grounded in individual liberty. To paraphrase Durkheim, a system that starts out by attempting to crack down on agreed-upon crimes with paternalistic and oppressive laws will likely lead to new crimes or criminals, because the paternalism will know no bounds. It eventually will undermine our culture's disposition and belief in liberty.

Durkheim described this logic in *Suicide,* a work, published in 1897, that remains one of the most comprehensive studies on the phenomenon. Durkheim found that in countries where married women had a difficult time obtaining a divorce, rates of suicide among those women were higher than in countries where divorces were easy to obtain. This suggested to him that a law intended to engender family cohesiveness could produce detrimental effects. He also realized that there were different types of suicide and cautioned that while a society might seek to prevent one type, the oppressive structure needed to accomplish that aim might only lead to still other types of suicide. Cladis tells us from his review of Durkheim's work that Durkheim was disturbed about abnormal rates of individualistic behavior (e.g., the gang member who cares little for the community in which he lives) but that he rejected the state, education, and religion as ways to curb this behavior.

I suspect Durkheim would have approved of Chuck's church, however, since it did not create informal control with religious ideology. The church provided a small group. Cladis says that Durkheim recognized that a unit "larger than the family but smaller than the political society, would be well suited for building centers of common life." It is the common life, more than law, that provides for resources that benefit us and for social sanctions that control us.

A communitarian-oriented crime-control picture is not as pleasant as strategies that do not rely on law. The important goals of public safety notwithstanding, time and time again I see neighbors supporting drug checkpoints, backing curfews, assisting in gang roundups, lobbying for "no loitering" laws, and trying to evict bothersome tenants. These are the options defined for them according to the narrowly conceptualized strategies usually put forth by the criminal justice system.

In the current process to build community, something disturbing happens: the power residing in communities slowly becomes subordinated and co-opted by well-intentioned agencies such as the police, planning boards, and legislatures. In the end, the powerful informal solutions residing in the abilities found only in those communities that face the problems dissipate or never receive the proper validation and resources to make them successful.

As Chuck tells me, if the purpose of the Gorge Act was "the greatest good for the greatest number"—preserving the gorge for generations to come at the cost of displacing a few local families or preventing development on local land—then everybody lost out. "The reality is that development skyrocketed after the act on unprotected land all along the gorge." By including Chuck's townsfolk in the process, public authority might have learned some valuable lessons and might have prevented mistakes. Instead, public authority served more powerful interests than just the greatest number.

As I described in my introduction, it is very hard to include gang members in any community-building process when they have been made the demons and the reason for so much of our public authority. Chuck's townsfolk became different demons, but demons nonetheless. They represented irrational, backwoods local interests trying to stymie the public good. The will of public authority failed to accommodate them adequately, and the legitimacy of that authority was undermined.

Some time later I enjoyed the occasion to talk with faculty members at Portland State University about some of the issues raised by Chuck. An urban planning professor, who I felt had been restlessly gauging my words, told me that the U.S. Forest Service did hold hearings and went out of its way to involve residents in the process. He wanted to know what more could the government have done. More than a decade after the Gorge Act the professor's words were shaped by insistence born of exasperation, and it was clear that resentment and indignation still existed on both sides. Communication had failed on a fundamental level from the start. Chuck told me that a public hearing was held by a U.S. senator but at the time (incredibly or conveniently, depending on where one stands) no one in the town knew about the meeting and no one attended. "Our congressman's office told us that the act was in committee and wouldn't come out. Less than a month later it did and he voted for it."

As a final insult to the legitimacy of public authority, or what little still existed in his town, Chuck noted that on paper the Gorge Act contained provisions for hardships, but that too was a myth in reality. The restrictions the act placed on the land meant that landowners who might have originally bought property for farming or other natural resources, or even to subdivide for other family members, were unable to use their property. Congress responded with a land-acquisition program that authorized the Forest Service to purchase those lands. According to Chuck, "70 to 80 percent of the first several millions of dollars were used to purchase property from the Trust for Public Lands in San Francisco. When I questioned the Forest Service about this in a public meeting I was ignored and later told their hands were tied by the designation of those funds by Congress to those purchases."

Far from representing irrational, backwoods, militia-oriented interests, Chuck's experience seems to be common in the Gorge Act process. Steven Klos, one of a group of twenty Gorge Scenic Area landowners, and Lauri Aunan, executive director of a two thousand–member group working to protect the gorge, jointly called on the government to do a better job of reaching out to landowners: "Although almost $40 million in federal money has been invested since 1986 to purchase more than 30,000 acres of sensitive property in the Gorge, thousands of acres remain to be purchased to fully achieve the Act's dual goals of providing fairness to landowners and protecting the most significant natural resources in the Gorge."

For law to lose its legitimacy is for law to lose its effect as a tool of social control. This, perhaps, is the most fundamental trap, and defect, with communitarian logic: the interdependent, safe community we seek on paper, or by law, will in practice be only as good as the integrity of the actors responsible for carrying out the intent of the law. If we rely too much on law as our problem solver and the actors responsible for application of the law fail, where do we turn to correct that failure—to more law? Do we seek better and more clever law when we ultimately seek to effect change in the behavior of those actors? The fundamental problem is probably related more to human behavior and relations than to our failure to craft loophole-free law.

≈ o ≈

Undermining the legitimacy of laws by increasing public authority seems a high price to pay. It is doubtful that any amount of public authority will ultimately make that housewife feel any better about black teens. Unless she gets to know the youths she fears and they become part of the community she experiences, all the laws in all the books will not lessen her fears. I am not sure that even with all the public authority in the world disposed against crime, every street corner would be safe for somebody's grandmother and every black man would regain his humanity. If the law is able to do these things, it will probably not do them well by attempting to control things that make citizens fearful. To control every potential threat through the law places legislatures in a legal arms race. Consider the attempts to control the use of curse words, computers, and even laser pointers (once popular for making presentations, their focused light beams are used by pranksters who wish to annoy others).

There is an alternative. Instead of law being used primarily as a reactive tool, as a response to threats and an exercise to predict and prevent wrongs, it might also help develop those elements and ensure those resources that make us a community. However, Durkheim's voice from more than a hundred years ago warns that state intervention to create community is an irony. It seems communitarians are an ironic lot. As Chuck's story illustrates, state intervention to create community is also paradoxical, in that such intervention can undermine community or place it in peril.

Alternatively, Richard Register and his supporters, worried about the potentially volatile impact of their fruit trees on bored teens, did not seek out the local city council to ban fruit picking and throwing. They talked to the teens and built a relationship. Katherine Anderson did not mobilize her community groups to expand hate-crime laws; she set out to create earnest and lasting dialogue in her community. These are only two examples of the stories we should know that describe the benefits in connecting and forming a community.

Conclusion

Beyond myths of the past to other strategies

"They, like, always have movies like that, where
some new teacher comes and everyone stops being a
gangsta and gets good grades and goes off to college."
"Yeah, why don't they have a real movie where no
one cares and students don't learn anything."
—MTV's Beavis and Butthead

Who better to speak to the "realness" of a lone teacher rehabilitating a throng of unruly classroom thugs than two of the most unruly, unreal characters in popular culture? It takes those two Attention Deficit Disorder–plagued, heavy-metal-loving, sex-crazed fictional teens to remind us that what is real is often—to paraphrase *The Velveteen Rabbit*—messy, well-worn, and imperfect. For community building to serve as a crime-control agenda, its construction will require grounding on a notion of justice more real than Hollywood myth, more dingy than flashy, high-tech crime-fighting tools, and more arduous than generating new laws and spending more money.

Community is a remarkable phenomenon dependent upon a sometimes bumpy, always ongoing process that takes energy, care, and attention. The key to community is sustained involvement, not temporary mobilization to address a threat. Most of all, community exists not in myths of the past but in the science of tomorrow. Community building as crime control is not just about understanding which strategies work and which fail to reduce crime. It is about which strategies value community and liberty, control and benevolence, and fashion relations that connect us rather than drive us further apart.

145

LESSONS FROM THE PAST

I am too young to know whether the past really offered that golden community complete with cohesive and interdependent residents who followed Victorian moral standards and obeyed cultural norms. I can, however, glimpse elements of that past. As my travels through the community-as-crime-control topography come to a close, I will begin to summarize a framework for tomorrow by first looking into the past and connecting what I see with what my travels have revealed. This view serves as a reminder that talk on building community must focus on uncovering tomorrow's hope, not yesterday's security.

There are lessons in the past. I learn those lessons on a savagely hot August day in eastern California. I think I understand this heat, or at least the raw inspiration it has provided in the creation of stirring myth. It is an unearthly heat. Flung from the dry, barren landscape, the heat whips sweat off my skin so quickly that only a brief tingle, a quick chill, offers relief before the air sends me wandering like a shark in a torrid, boiling ocean. To stop moving is to feel it surround, engulf, and suffocate me. I try to endure the searing air just a few more moments before retreating to the relief offered by my car's air conditioner.

I am a few miles south of Independence, California, among scrub and barren soil that is either too rocky to till or too sandy to hold water. I stand in the midst of sprawling acreage in Owens Valley in the eastern Sierra Nevada, an area that is known as Manzanar. Once a thriving pear and apple growing center, before the water here was diverted to Los Angeles to supply a thirsty, growing metropolis, Manzanar is now a desert best known as the site of a World War II relocation center. Manzanar was one of ten camps in the United States that interned more than one hundred thousand Americans during the war.

From my vantage in Owens Valley, I can see snow patches along the craggy eastern Sierra Nevada range. What a painful tease they must have been to the involuntary visitors here more than fifty years ago. The cool, snowcapped peaks, though visible through the barbed-wire fencing, were as out of reach as democracy and liberty were to the ten thousand internees held in Manzanar.

Few visual reminders of what was once here exist. The barracks have been dismantled, the wood sold to build homes for returning GIs. The roads are overgrown and broken up, the foundations covered with windblown soil. A graveyard remains, but most of its buried were long ago disinterred and moved to other sites. The remnants of Japanese rock gardens hide among a few oak trees that dot the landscape.

There is, however, a lesson for our times that this forsaken world compels me to seek. A few weeks later, as I dig through news stories on congressional hearings held to decide whether reparations should be paid to the families of Americans held at places like Manzanar, I come across a statement made by former Supreme Court justice Arthur Goldberg. At the time of the internment, few stopped to ask whether it was "legally and morally wrong," Goldberg said. Instead they rallied around slogans and did the unthinkable because, as a former justice department official noted of the times, "We were all frightened, we were all scared."

The lessons continue. When Americans were interned, War Relocation Administration (WRA) officials were lambasted for coddling and overfeeding the prisoners. The WRA was also chastised when the public learned that the camps would someday release their prisoners. Some WRA officials even justified the internment as "retribution" for the attack on Pearl Harbor.

During the internment the *Christian Science Monitor* was the only mainstream American publication to speak out against the practice on a regular basis. Most popular magazines reported on how the internees were adapting to new schooling and work programs. The federal government sponsored research to test, among other things, how well the camps were educating the children of captives and what new techniques might produce better citizens in captivity.

Back at Manzanar, as the loose, rocky soil crunches under my feet, I realize I am walking on the remnants of a road. Time has softened the hard outlines of this sprawling complex. So too has time softened the images most of us maintain of the past. Some authors have suggested that America would never build another Manzanar because we have created greater freedoms and civil liberties than we had then. However, this freedom brings new dangers, such as a society faced with self-interested, expressive behavior and lacking a shared moral value. I am not convinced that another Manzanar is completely improbable in America.

My lack of conviction stems from what I have seen in my travels. I have seen how fear rocks our communities. Two generations ago it was fear of Japanese Americans. Nearly one generation ago, it was a nuclear holocaust. Only tomorrow will today's fear come to light: Is it immigrants, crime and victimization, infectious disease, the new millennium? The efforts to build community that I witnessed were more like reactions to current fears than a focus on how creating community, by connecting with one another, ultimately enriches us emotionally, physically, and economically. A community so enriched is able to benefit from "collective efficacy" and thus, as a by-product, will be less racked by crime. But tackling crime should not remain the only, or even the primary, aim of community building, because then our fears become our guiding ambitions. When fear guides us, Manzanars are possible.

Each generation faces fears and uncertainties, seemingly inescapable problems and burdens. My visit to Manzanar comforts me with the realization that even the worst fears of the moment will someday pass. Yet the injustices allowed to occur in response to these fears—the segregation of people, the concentration of power—leave a legacy that is not always easy to repair. I do not believe it takes intellectual gymnastics to see a disturbing similarity between the history of government-supported research of internment camps and the current research focus on crime-control strategies.

The boosterism that went on in support of internment camps and the boosterism that supports community policing, order-maintenance policing, and Crime Prevention through Environmental Design parallel each other. Some Japanese Americans thought it best for the country that their government place them in camps, just as some inner-city residents think it best for their neighborhoods that they endure checkpoints, citizen patrols, sweeps, crackdowns, and raids.

Far removed from the moment, just as I was physically removed from my friend Bill's limited intervention in that heartland city, Americans cannot always understand. We often make the mistake of asking how 1940s America could intern its own because of their race, or how Germans could look the other way during Nazi atrocities. Perhaps a more useful question would emerge if we remind ourselves that we all suffer, and benefit, from our moment in time. Our moment is as inescapable as the heat in Owens Valley, so we must live with it by reacting to it in one manner or another. This is another lesson from Manzanar: we are beings who react to social moments. If we can allow ourselves some curiosity and humility, and the feelings associated with uncomfortable cognitive dissonance, we might ask, What are we *now* doing that generations in the future will view as horrendous acts on a par with interning our own citizens?

One of the recurring themes that emerged in my travels is that the community project is pursued with the best of intentions, and people are working hard to build community and to respond to crime. But even if such a project is given every opportunity to work, there is still a disturbing tension underlying it. It is a tension about division between race and class, about using community to oil the cogs of a punitive criminal justice system and about locking people away rather than forging new relations with one another as the most important problem-solving strategy.

That we must endure these disturbing tensions in community building, I believe, results from our overreliance on criminal justice means to address social ills. There is enough blame to go around. Conservatives defend personal responsibility and self-governance but then take credit for controlling crime with intrusive, top-down governmental strategies. Liberals argue for systemic change but focus on saving individual actors from the demons in their past by treating them or rehabilitating them. Both sides touch on the answer but miss the important part. Community as crime control is the ultimate conservative agenda, in that it relies on bottom-up, community-based informal social control with little regard for state intervention. Community as crime control is also the ultimate liberal agenda, because it relies more on changing systemic influences and correcting flaws holistically, and much less on correcting individual actors within those communities who are just elements within a social dynamic.

As I demonstrated in chapters 5 and 6, humans are actors embedded in social relations and their environments. Connection is about establishing those relations. A common libertarian and conservative argument suggests that to attribute crime to systemic or community-based influences deprives a person of his or her humanity, free will, and personal responsibility. I think this argument misses something important. To point to community-based reasons for crime reminds us of our humanity. We are a species that, since the dawn of time, has relied on the mutual support of its members for survival. We are humans because, when we choose to, we can accommodate one another, and we can easily find ourselves able to create community in the most inhospitable of climates. This is the final lesson I discovered at Manzanar.

I leave the inhospitable desert ghost camp and visit the county archives in Independence, where I find evidence that behind the barbed-wire fences and guard towers, community thrived, providing a culturally rich oasis in the desert. Those Americans of Japanese descent who were vilified by their nation, removed from their homes, separated from their pasts, and deprived of their businesses did not give up on their humanity. Instead they forged new relations, built new connections, and created a community that overcame their loneliness, buffered their anger, and kept them sane. People everywhere have the ability to create community. If certain groups of people are denied a place in the larger community—be they urban teens or rural ranchers—they will still form communities, such as gangs or militias, even if those communities may ultimately threaten the larger community.

Crime control by connecting is no more about denying people their humanity than it is about finding a way to make the machine of criminal justice run more smoothly. I have returned to this theme time and time again because it was a recurrent one in my travels.

Current efforts to build community invariably anoint an arrest-centered criminal justice enterprise rather than reestablish connections and resources within and across communities.

Consider that in *Fixing Broken Windows,* George Kelling and Catherine Coles include a chapter titled "The Importance of Connecting" to demonstrate that when the police know members in their community, they have an easier time policing. As Kelling and Coles tell it, "Things happen when police officers get out of their cars and systematically interact with citizens, through foot patrol or some other tactic." The example they provide comes from Kelling's days walking the beat in Newark, New Jersey, back in the mid-1970s: "This was a time when most of the citizens in the area were black and the officers were white, when memories of the 1960s riots in American cities were still fresh." Officers in this example "moved easily along city streets, chatted with citizens, explained to miscreants why they had to behave, ordered people to 'move on,' and occasionally, made arrests." That they did this was a result of "an authority negotiated as citizens and police came to know and trust each other and to recognize their mutual interest in maintaining order on the streets."

What specific occurrence do Kelling and Coles hold up as a prime example of what happens when citizens connect with police? Two officers arrested a "drunk African-American man" who had been harassing a "terrified . . . African-American woman with a young child at a bus stop." Because the officers knew the drunk man's name, they could address him and at first offer to leave him alone if he would just walk away. When the subject refused to move on, the "officers immediately grabbed [him], wrestled him to the ground, handcuffed him, and called for a car to take him to the station for booking." Even though the car took twenty minutes to arrive, people in the neighborhood did not question the officers' tactics. One officer forcibly held the subject on the ground while another officer "exchanged comments with citizens."

According to Kelling and Coles, the man's "street colleagues never came to his aid, but ridiculed him for behaving as he had." Finally, Kelling and Coles suggest, "How different this event might have been if the officers and citizens had been unfamiliar with each other. For many white officers, making such an arrest on a Newark street, when the vast majority of passersby were African Americans, would have been a nightmare scenario."

The issue raised by this example, coupled with my reflections on Manzanar, is that even if policing occurred in the past by some agreed-upon standard, this history does not make the practice right. It is difficult to tell whether Kelling and Coles were witnessing citizens of a past Newark agreeing with the force of law in their lives or whether they were witnessing citizens' acquiescence to an overwhelming power and a lack of their own power to prevent intrusion by the police. As a Spokane community program director, quoted in an earlier chapter, said, people live in the latter state for only so long. The neighborhood activist in Santa Ana noted that the police practice of rounding up gang kids in the middle of the night might not irk residents so much if those residents were resigned to that tactic as the only problem-solving tool. What happens when those same residents desire to share a standard of public conduct but grow tired of seeing police arrest as the likely avenue to solving their problems?

I explained in chapter 3 that police officers who continually apply more force to a problem do not always reap the benefits that such an application might seem to offer. Some residents in Spokane's east-central neighborhoods grew tired of problem-solving resources going into the patrols of retired white neighbors, even though the police went to great lengths, with upwards of twenty-eight community-based programs, to connect with the community. Kelling and Coles, as well as many police reformers and policy makers, miss the real importance of connecting because they never articulate strategies to increase a variety of neighborhood and community resources that will establish informal social control in communities.

On one level Kelling and Coles's evidence raises a concern for the loss of an agreed-upon standard of public conduct, the same loss I mentioned in chapter 4. At the same time, angry mobs of black residents questioning what police are doing to a subject need to be appreciated for what they are: evidence that there is unhappiness with both police tactics and arrest as the tool of choice a society uses to confront social ills. I am concerned by this because if there is a lack of shared meaning about public behavior, it is not because certain segments of a society have dropped the ball while others hold true to some moral standard.

I hope my travels have demonstrated that if there is a lack of shared meaning about public behavior, it is not because it *cannot* exist. Powerful and shared values do exist. Consumption, shopping, and mall life form one such shared norm. Certain segments of the society do not, however, engage in community life. One reason is that those segments are indirectly prevented from taking part in a community process that will allow that shared value to develop. Thus, because crime-control policies do not exploit exchange, communication, dialogue, feedback, and connections, those policies fail to establish shared public-behavior values.

By shared value I do not mean, as Cheryl Steele expressed in a previous chapter, Class A taking responsibility for Class B's moral education. Planner Wendy Sarkissian and her colleagues tested "social mixing" as a way for the middle class to "raise standards by nurturing a spirit of emulation" on the part of the lower class. Effects of that type of social mixing, along with efforts to create diversity and "cross-cultural fertilization," have been inconclusive and often contradictory. The effective community project is born from partnership, not patriarchy, and nourished by equal voice, not preferred opinion.

THE FUTURE

Any strategy to combat this lack of shared value and the frustration with police should not seek to restore compliance with the police simply for its own sake, as police reformers and academic theorists all too often suggest. A strategy that is agreeable to all is a strategy born of consensus and hence a strategy that will foster compliance. In reviewing the evidence gathered from my travels, I have devised one such strategy that emphasizes connection as an important tool, not because it smoothes the job police have to do in arresting people, but because it changes the very conception of what is efficacious in restoring community strength and controlling crime.

One objective of this book has been to argue for an alternative view on crime control. I devote the remaining few pages to playing with a potential future strategy as one of many possible conceptual tools. It is a strategy that emphasizes law as an important conveyor of society's norms and standards and worthy of enforcement. The enforcement of law, however, comes not through the threat of force but through building relations culturally and spatially, by fostering community and its resultant informal social control through forging relations.

I develop a working outline for this strategy by using two hypothetical situations potentially faced by any community. Indeed, both of these situations are composites of events that occurred in cities I visited. In explaining how to respond to these situations, I borrow from the preceding chapters and use additional data from the field.

> ■ A state prison places a child molester on parole and releases him to his mother's residence in a middle-class, suburban neighborhood. Children walk by the house as they go to and from school and play on the street fronting the residence.

A probation officer told me that one complication in community-based crime prevention or response is dealing with criminals: they are the dirty part of the process no one wants to admit. Nowhere is this detail more evident than with sexual predators who prey on children. Treatment for such offenders has not proven itself, and neighborhood residents would rather turn to vigilantism than live near a sexual offender. Children deserve environments in which they can engage in "unrestricted free play," as the *San Jose Mercury News* has advised, but few children growing up in contemporary urban and suburban America experience such environments.

Whether guided by fear or ambition, more than ever before parents direct nearly all their children's time, taking them to soccer matches, piano lessons, school events, and friends' homes. Children need the cognitive development that arises from experimenting, solving problems on their own, and occasionally getting in trouble, but they must always learn without risking attack by a neighborhood resident.

Leaders can take a positive approach, as Police Chief Jon Walters did, by supporting neighborhood meetings to exchange dialogue about sexual predators in their cities, not mobilizations to sweep those offenders under the proverbial carpet, away from the watchful eye of the community. Residents can take a positive approach, as Cheryl Steele's neighbors did, by confronting the molester with creative suggestions that attempt to keep him under informal community social control.

Cheryl Steele's neighbors actually did meet with a molester and his mother. At the meeting they agreed upon some conditions intended to prevent the molester from harming children in the future. He agreed to hang a yellow placard on his door whenever he was at home. Parents instructed neighborhood children to keep away from the house anytime the placard was present. Parents told children that the neighbor was sick and that the placard was his way of telling the neighborhood he needed "quiet time." Residents agreed to make visits to the molester's residence on a regular basis, and the molester agreed to take a polygraph test at the residents' insistence should the need arise.

I am uneasy with the reliance on the polygraph to ease neighborhood concerns, only because it is a flawed tool. Strategies to prevent a child molester from reoffending need not rely on polygraphs. The important point is that through neighborhood meetings, the residents can confront their fear and give it a name and a face. Suddenly such a fear becomes manageable. By being able to discuss and confront the issue, neighbors also make it possible that the molester may turn to one of them should he find himself under stress or afraid of violating his parole. He can turn to them believing they will help him stay the course, not run him out of town to an unknown place where he will likely reoffend. The approach in this case is grounded on law enforcement that keeps the offender under control by stabilizing his environment and by making him want to stay in a place where he is kept under the watchful, but not too intrusive, eyes of his community.

■ A police department wishes to implement a crime-prevention program that changes norms and behaviors and draws on community informal social control.

It would seem that police departments already have such programs in place. Programs such as DARE are designed to introduce a zero-tolerance norm for drug use among school-age children. Earlier

I briefly touched on the more than two dozen programs in Spokane, including one to reward cooperative behavior among neighborhood residents. Unfortunately, DARE has not lived up to its billing and, as I noted earlier, the programs in Spokane did not alleviate tensions in certain neighborhoods. Of even greater concern is the inability these programs have to change the perceptions of officers (such as the recruit in Oregon) on what it takes to police and to reach community members (such as those park visitors in Arizona) who are not currently violating laws but could nevertheless add to the power of the community project by sharing community values about public behavior and cooperation.

A future approach might recognize that doing and connecting will change norms more than thinking and educating. When cities or neighborhoods develop relations across disparate groups, improvements can occur. John Dombrink, a University of California criminologist, describes programs that the San Francisco Police Department implemented following several high-profile problems during the 1980s. Officers now attend peer-group sessions on ethics, sergeants conduct weekly evaluations to reward positive behavior, and "gripe sessions" are operated with local community leaders.

During my stay at Indiana University, I found the administration aggressively addressing date rape by increasing communication across groups on either side of the issue. In fraternities, where organizational isolation often breeds a mentality conducive to date rape, officials sponsored awareness training and frank discussion of the topic. In these discussions potential "rapists" might openly discuss their attitudes with potential "victims" and advocates from rape prevention centers. Portland's Katherine Anderson tackled hate crime in a similar fashion, by avoiding name-calling and blame but offering all sides a voice and the opportunity to seek serious answers to their questions, no matter how racist, sexist, or criminally minded those questions might first appear to her. These are all important interventions that refute the popular maxim "Talk is cheap." Open, honest, and nonjudgmental talk that gives even the most alienated and despised room to receive social connection and feedback is an important and yet underemployed strategy in eliminating the horrendous crimes that take place in contemporary America.

Some authors, myself included, have noted that if police are to pursue norm changes in communities, they must also achieve those changes in their own house. The recruit in Oregon could hardly conceptualize how he might creatively handle a dog urinating on a resident's lawn when his field training officer was assessing him by a fairly rigid and outdated norm based on arrest and assertiveness. In the police subculture, administrations seldom admit to systemic problems. When faced with problems, administrators often resort to solving them as they would deal with crime, by invoking authority and the hierarchical structuring of power or by pointing to a few rogue cops. Not only will change be less likely to appear in such an atmosphere, but corruption, scandal, and abuse will likely continue.

Airline piloting was once a profession, like policing, that was modeled after a military chain of command in which the captain held ultimate authority. *Condé Nast Traveler* reports that such a cultural model in the cockpit is potentially deadly, because a captain's error may not be questioned by the junior officers. Nearly half the accidents studied by the National Transportation Safety Board in 1994 resulted from the first officer's "failure to challenge a captain's action." A new strategy called Cockpit Resource Management "teaches captains to share authority with their junior officers, and first officers to assert themselves." They are seen as social equals rather than people of different rank, and junior officers are encouraged to improvise problem solving in the cockpit.

Police departments could learn a lot from airline strategies. Departments that design and lead top-down educational programs to prevent crime by telling students or community members what is the right thing to do would be better served by encouraging practices and communication that validate the students' or community members' concerns. Such a process not only prevents potential trouble within departments but also can allow for the emergence of shared values.

"A civic culture is a body of narratives," observes political philosopher Thomas Bridges. Creating that civic culture requires individuals to be treated as free and equal but also to be able to "step out of perspectives from which they normally view the world, and see things from a different point of view." Evidence from chapter 7 suggests that officers' or educators' telling, warning, or threatening people such as gang members about how they should behave is a poor substitute for sponsoring sessions in which people from a variety of backgrounds can get to know one another and work to resolve their needs and fears by building upon social networks. For the suburban home owner the issue may be fear for her safety. For the gang member it may be a need for belonging and for future opportunities. Future strategies can expand the reach of informal social networks capable of addressing those fears and needs.

SUMMARY

I have presented only two brief examples as a way to explain how a new conceptual tool might be used to deal with crime control through the establishment of community. There are other areas I neglected to address, such as planning and legislation. The same theoretical approach applies to those areas. As I mentioned in the previous chapter, honoring the potential crime-control power that resides in community is achieved less by attempting to suppress every potential harmful act with draconian measures, and more by developing those elements and ensuring those resources that build relations, ties, and networks.

Any conceptual tool, study, program, or policy designed to draw on the power indigenous to a community must avoid the defects found in the programs of the places I visited. A policy designed to curb crime based on some "community" model can too readily drive community apart rather than bring it together, if that policy does not strive to foster strong, long-term relations among all entities in a community. A society such as ours, peopled by a transient citizenry, has a government that can maintain the static structures needed to allow relations to flourish as people enter and leave communities.

Governments do pursue other paths, but I am not sure those paths offer the same hope. More aggressive policing may very well put a dent in crime. Citizen mobilization may close crack houses, stop prostitution, and cajole kids into behaving. Laws dictating how we should act and behave at every stage in our life may bring about more prosocial behavior. Perfectly controlled and designed environments may provide the appearance of safety, tidiness, and success.

However, citizen mobilization around crime lasts only as long as the threat exists; a need for community is continual. There are tremendous economic costs in waging a war against all for our safety, tremendous social costs in seeing certain races and classes of people as a threat requiring control.

The community that matters most is the one in which police are a limited outside entity, mobilization is a simple daily communication with neighbors we know, and a multitude of laws are unnecessary. This is not a nostalgic image of the past as much as an appeal to reshape our culture and our thinking toward an entirely new conception. What matters is viewing our individuality as formed by our social space, our communities. The irony is that when people (the social) matter, it is much easier to be an individual. When individuals matter most, people cannot exist.

≈ o ≈

Because it is our culture, and all its varied manifestations, that must ultimately provide the support for the role our social lives play in our destiny, I have relied on cultural references throughout this book. Through these cultural representations, ranging from discussions on architecture to quotations from cartoons, I have attempted to demonstrate the tensions that underlie our contemporary existence: We are individuals, yet we long for something more social. We speak loudly against antisocial behavior through our laws and punitive justice system yet still remain unsettled about the prospect of injustices and the violation of civil liberties.

In one final reference from popular culture, I look to Orson Welles, who brilliantly articulated this tension in his 1958 classic *Touch of Evil*. In the film, an honest, hardworking Mexican justice official (played by a likable though implausible Charlton Heston) thwarts a corrupt border-town police captain involved in planting evidence against a suspect. When confronted, the captain groans that the Mexican official "doesn't care if killers hang or not so long as we obey the fine print in the rule books." The official replies, "I don't think police should work like dogcatchers putting criminals behind bars." The captain interrupts with, "Our job is tough enough," to which the official proclaims, "It's supposed to be tough, it has to be tough. A policeman's job is only easy in a police state—that's the whole point, captain!"

That is the whole point indeed. There is community building that is easy. The stories I came to know during my travels about further class separation and race divisions, about greater police influence and heightened alienation, might become *our* story if we settle for the easy route. But there are other stories I also came to know. These stories illuminated a difficult route but a more profitable one. They were about understanding community building and people power by first finding ideas in diverse places, even among leaders, and then allowing ourselves the capacity to seek alternatives in our crime-control saga. They told of community building by creating structures that involve humans and by seeing the police as facilitators and enablers but not problem solvers. They provided glimpses of community building that overcame separation rather than increasing it. They illustrated how we must remain aware of how space and connection can influence behavior, and how place might foster problem-solving skills indigenous to communities of people. If community building as crime control is to become *our* story, it is up to all of us to reach for something more, no matter how tough it is. That is the whole point.

Notes

All notes are cross-referenced to correspond to the book page number in which the citation or quote appears. A selected bibliography follows this section. A reference not cited in this note section refers to the general thrust of the entire work and can be found in the selected bibliography.

Introduction

5   Sampson has written extensively on informal social control in neighborhoods. He coined "collective efficacy" in Sampson et al. (1997), p. 919. See also Sampson (1995, 1993, 1991).

6   "Nostalgic pining," "Must spring from": Cladis (1992), p. 76.

7   Shaw and McKay's dismay with the Chicago Area Project is discussed more specifically in Schlossman (1983).

10   The *Michigan Law Review* issue referred to is vol. 87, no. 8, 1989.

11   Cornel West's remarks are from "Toward an End to Racism and Prejudice," a speech made at the U.S. Holocaust Memorial Museum "Visions of the 21st Century" Program, Washington, D.C., January 13, 1996.

15   "Most police work," "What the proponents": Wilson (1970), pp. 286, 288.

16   Skolnick and Fyfe (1993), p. 165, note that to counter Operation Rescue activity, council member Michael Woo spearheaded a drive by the council to pass a "resolution urging the LAPD to engage in 'vigorous enforcement' at Rescue demonstrations."

16   Trojanowicz discusses the youths in the park in Trojanowicz and Bucqueroux (1990).

1. *Mayberry versus Starsky and Hutch*

22 "Which are not," "This style," "Almost invariably": Wilson (1970), pp. 200, 180, 200.

23 "Juveniles, Negroes, drunks": Wilson (1970), p. 170.

27 The ACLU's evidence on NYPD tactics was discussed by Norman Siegel, executive director of the New York American Civil Liberties Union, at the forum "Crime and Punishment in the U.S.," sponsored by the *New Yorker* magazine and the New York City Bar Association, New York, February 18, 1997.

27 McNamara is quoted in Christopher John Farley, "A Beating in Brooklyn: New York's Finest Come Under Fire after a Haitian Man Is Sexually Assaulted, Allegedly by Cops," *Time*, August 25, 1997.

31 "We know her," "She could not," "Young woman": Didion (1992), pp. 253, 258, 258.

2. No Humans Involved

38 "Message from your NRO": COPS—*Southeast Courier*, vol. 3, July 1996, p. 1.

40 Spokane police chief and car occupants: *Spokane Spokesman-Review*, July 17, 1996, sec. B, p. 3, col. 1.

43 The Houston patrol time study is referred to in Kessler (1993).

44 Chief Walters is quoted in Jeff Collins, "Attacking Crime from All Fronts, Safely: Santa Ana's Winning Battle against Crime Relies on Several Police Strategies and Programs," *Orange County Register*, February 11, 1996, Metro sec., p. 7, col. 1.

3. Spy Shops and Nasty Old People

50 The references to Metzger's WAR group are culled from several sources. A cogent analysis is provided electronically by the Southern Poverty Law Center, http://www.splcenter.org/legalaction/1a-3.html (April 24, 1999)and http://www.nizkor.org/ s.vv. *Nazi holocaust, Holocaust, Tom Metzger* (June 12, 1998).

67 "According to researchers": Smith and Davis (1993) and McMillan et al. (1995).

4. Incivilities and Shared Conceptions

69   Fost, "Fairfax Community Exercise Reveals Humanity's Dark Side," *Marin Independent Journal,* July 13, 1997, sec. C, p. 1.

70   The social hygiene movement is referred to in Liss and Schlossman (1984).

73   "Portland's 'white trash enclave'": http://www.monk.com/ ontheroad/portland/pdxguide/guide.html (April 24, 1999). Monk notes that the southeast neighborhoods still provide "a slice of cheap and satisfying Southeast white trash in the far reaches of the rapidly gentrifying Northwest," and that "Southeast Portland divides into two unique camps — the aging hippie/feminist/slacker crowd along Hawthorne between 30th and 40th Streets and the more bizarre element found in the far reaches of the area (referred to as Deep Southeast by those in the know), which is essentially a white trash enclave with by far the weirdest, wackiest, seediest assortment of people and businesses in the Great Northwest."

76–77   "As members of societies": Laszlo et al. (1996), p. 34.

77   "It is easier": ibid., p. 5.

78   "Relying upon": Skogan (1990), p. 157.

78   Verba's findings are in Verba et al. (1993), p. 307.

78–79   Perkins's data are in Perkins et al. (1996), p. 90.

79   "Behavior settings": Taylor (1997), p. 119.

79   "Set of shared symbols": Laszlo et al. (1996), p. 66.

81   The analysis of black buying power is in "Blacks Spending More Money: Study," *Jet,* September 9, 1996, p. 40.

81   "We consume too much": Sagoff (1997), p. 96.

5. Scene of the Crime

89   "Because economic and military success": Boyd and Richerson (1990), pp. 113, 124 The term "culturally endogamous" is from ibid., p. 122.

90   Aronson's comments are in Aronson (1988).

92   Sarkissian's theory is in Sarkissian et al. (1990).

92   "The last third": Friedman (1985), p. 503.

93   "Buildings are," "the original bank": Sullivan, quoted in Frei (1992), pp. 204, 171.

93   "Sullivan had a blind spot": Kunstler (1993), p. 67.

94   See discussions on Sullivan's papers in Duncan (1965), Frei (1992), Andrew (1985), and Sullivan (1979).

94   For my examination of community policing, see DeLeon-Granados (1997).

94–95   Kunstler's descriptions are in Kunstler (1993), p. 82.

95   "In our democratic land": Sullivan was speaking before the American Architect Association; his speech was published in *American Contractor* (1906). See Sullivan (1979), p. 229.

95–96   Jacobs's comment is from Jacobs (1961), p. 13.

96   "Defensible space" comes from Newman (1972).

96   "When common spaces": Newman, http://www.huduser.org/rrr/newman.html s.vv. *Newman, Defensible Space* (April 21, 1999).

97   The U.S. Department of Housing and Urban Development provides an electronic dissemination of its reports at http://www.huduser.org.

98   Newman, http://www.huduser.org/rrr/newman.html (April 21, 1999).

98   "Defensible Space has been misinterpreted": Newman, ibid.

98   The information about the Royal Canadian Mounted Police is in Felson (1994), p. 123.

99   Felson's arguments are in ibid., pp. 2–3.

99   Felson's remarks about glorifying informal social control are in ibid., pp. 34–35.

102–3   "Releaser cues" and subsequent Zimbardo remarks are in Zimbardo (1969), pp. 287–92.

103   Kelling is quoted in Farley, "A Beating in Brooklyn."

104   The Department of Justice handbook is Rubenstein et al. (1980), p. 61.

105   "Attendant determinism": Soja (1992), p. 122.

6. New Urbanism

106   "Distinctive and beloved landmark": Jacobs (1961), p. 386.

108–9   "Bad neighborhoods": von Hoffman, "Good News: From Boston to San Francisco the Community-Based Housing Move- ment Is Transforming Bad Neighborhoods," *Atlantic,* January 1997, pp. 31–35.

109 Katz's remarks are quoted by Mark Faber in "Starbucks Nation," *Seattle Weekly,* February 19, 1997, p. 23.

109 "Recycled homes": Florence Williams, "Retread Rebel: New Age Developer Builds 'Earthships' — and Raises Ire — with Old Tires," *San Francisco Chronicle,* September 1, 1997, sec. A, p. 3, col. 1.

110 The reunion is described in Darrell Satzman, "Reunion Recalls the Dawn of Suburbia," *Los Angeles Times,* October 26, 1997.

111 "In an effort": Dade Hayes, "Juvenile Crime Will Be Topic of Hearing," *Los Angeles Times,* October 25, 1997.

111 The Irvine experiment is described in *Lotus International,* no. 89, May 1996, pp. 7–99.

112 "Community Truly a 'Haven' Town Perfect for Hit Movie and Residents," *Florida Times-Union,* July 6, 1998, Metro sec.

114 "Heteroglossia": Davis (1992), p. 260; "belief in suburbia": Soja (1992); "NIMBY syndrome": Castells (1991), p. 19; "edge cities": Garreau (1991).

114 "Just as white suburbanites" and subsequent *Economist* quotes: "Doomed to Burn? Solving the Problems of Poor Inner Cities," *Economist,* vol. 323, 1992, pp. 21–25.

115 "Each step": Woodward, Associated Press wire service, Sep- tember 6, 1997.

116 "The compact settlement" and subsequent quotes in this para- graph are from Gordon and Richardson (1997).

120 "Developers are": ibid.

120 "Jive-plastic colonials": Kunstler (1993), p. 10.

120 Dream houses are described in an editorial preface to "The Renovation Report," *Metropolitan Home,* vol. 29, no. 5 (1997), p. 131.

121 Jencks's comments are in Jencks (1993), p. 93.

121 Gehry's interview was broadcast as "Revolution in a Box" on *Nightline,* October 6, 1997. He was hailed as the world's fore- most contemporary architect in this segment.

7. The Power of Connection

123–24   "Virtually limitless potential" and other Zimbardo comments are in Zimbardo (1969), p. 240.

124   "Obligations, liabilities": ibid., p. 248.

124   "The hypocrisy": ibid., p. 242.

125   "Deindividuation": ibid., p. 248.

125–26   "With numbing regularity": Milgram (1965), p. 57. See also Milgram (1963).

126   "Delusions of," "Obedience requires": Zimbardo (1974), p. 566.

126   "Individual uniqueness," "When a dehumanized": Zimbardo (1969), p. 304.

126   "Resist urban planning": ibid., p. 305.

127   Tilly and Bearman's arguments are from http://eclectic.ss. uci.edu/~drwhite s.vv. *Tilly, Bearman* (December 3, 1997).

128   Granovetter's conclusions are in Granovetter (1973); a discussion of Gans's work is in ibid., p. 360.

128   Neal's remarks are in Neal (1971), pp. 111, 110.

129   "Urban and metropolitan": Johnson (1995), p. 77.

129   "Poetry is the last": Castells (1991), p. 20.

129   "We are moral beings": Durkheim is quoted in Jacoby (1994), p. 247.

8. Communitarianism

133   "Communicate and symbolize," "is a common response": Ross (1996), s.v. *Communitarianism.*

133   "The communitarian movement": Richard John Neuhaus, "The Communities Missing from 'Communitarianism,'" *First Things,* February 1994, pp. 48–60 (http://www.firstthings. com/ftissues/ft9402/ public.html#missing [April 28, 1999]).

133–34   "Riders have a duty," "promotes an effort": Ross (1996).

134   "An energetic": Cladis (1992), p. 91.

134   "Might read something like this": ibid.

134   "Contested concept": Spence (1994).

134   "The liberal vocabulary": Cladis (1992), p. 2.

135   "Takes on a myriad": ibid., p. 91.

135   "Plato's cave": ibid., p. 93.

136–37   "Potentially fatal weakness": Neuhaus, "The Communities Missing."

137   "Pay almost no attention," "it is often": Joshua Abramowitz, "The Tao of Community" (review of Etzioni's *Spirit of Community*), *Public Interest*, no. 113 (1993), pp. 119–22, as cited in Neuhaus, "The Communities Missing."

137   "For communitarianism" and subsequent quotes from *First Things:* Neuhaus, "The Communities Missing."

140   "Desires and reasons": Cladis (1992), p. 19.

141   Cladis's review of Durkheim's work is in ibid., p. 65.

141   "Larger than the family": ibid., p. 76.

142–43   "Although almost $40 million": Steven J. Klos and Lauri G. Aunan, "Protecting the Gorge and Its Landowners," *Seattle Times,* September 11, 1997, editorial, p. B5.

Conclusion

147   "Legally and morally wrong," "We were all frightened": Congressional Hearings of the Commission on Wartime Relocation, as reported by United Press International, July 15, 1981.

147   Criticisms of the WRA are in ibid.; the "justification" is in ibid., November 3, 1981.

·147   "The only mainstream American publication": My perspective on which publications spoke out against internment comes from a review of legal and trade periodicals from 1940 to 1950. Only the *Nation,* the *New Republic,* and the *Christian Science Monitor* ran regular criticisms. *Time, Reader's Digest, Newsweek,* and *Life* all covered issues like "Educating for Victory" and shifted their tone only as time wore on. Worse, academic and government research focused on such issues as "Education behind Barbed Wire," *Survey Midmonthly* 80: 347–49; "Community Activities in War Relocation Centers in Arkansas," *Recreation* 38:261–65; "Cooperative Community Program at Manzanar," *Educating for Victory* 2:30–43; and "Health Education in a War Relocation Project: Poston, Arizona," *Public Health* 33:357–61.

151–52   "Things happen" and subsequent quotes in the next several paragraphs: Kelling and Coles, http://www.theatlantic.com/ search/ s.vv. *Connecting, Fixing Broken Windows.*

153   "Raise standards, "cross-cultural fertilization": Sarkissian et al. (1990), p. 13.

154   "Unrestricted free play": Sue Hutchinson, "Youngsters' Carefree Days Are No More," *San Jose Mercury News,* February 4, 1997.

156   Dombrink's descriptions are in Dombrink (1993), p. 387.

157   "Failure to challenge," "teaches captains": P. Garrison, "Can Culture Cause a Crash?" *Condé Nast Traveler,* July 1997, pp. 23–28.

157   "A civic culture," "step out": Bridges (1994), p. 25.

Selected Bibliography

Andrew, D. (1985). *Louis Sullivan and the Polemics of Modern Architecture*. Urbana: University of Illinois Press.

Aronson, E. (1988). *The Social Animal*. Palo Alto: Stanford University Press.

Associated Press. Community Truly a "Haven" Town Perfect for Hit Movie and Residents (1998). *Florida Times-Union,* July 6, Metro sec. Cambridge, Mass.: Northern Light Technology LLC.

Boyd, R., and P. J. Richerson (1990). Culture and Cooperation. In J. Mansbridge (ed.), *Beyond Self-Interest*. Chicago: University of Chicago Press.

Bridges, T. (1994). *The Culture of Citizenship: Inventing Postmodern Civic Culture*. Albany: State University of New York Press.

Castells, M. (1991). *The Informational City: A New Framework for Social Change*. The City in the 1990s Series, lecture 3. Toronto: Centre for Urban and Community Studies.

Cladis, M. S (1992). *A Communitarian Defense of Liberalism: Emile Durkheim and Contemporary Social Theory*. Palo Alto: Stanford University Press.

Davis, M. (1992). *City of Quartz*. New York: Vintage.

DeLeon-Granados, W. (1997). Nightsticks to Knighthood: A Case for Articulation of Community Policing's Divergent Themes. *Policing: An International Journal of Police Strategy and Management* 20:374–91.

Delgado, R. (1989). Storytelling for Oppositionists and Others: A Plea for Narrative. *Michigan Law Review* 87:2411–41.

Didion, J. (1993). *After Henry*. New York: Vintage.

Dombrink, J. (1993). The Touchables: Vice and Police Corruption in the 1980's. In H. N. Pontell (ed.), *Social Deviance*. Englewood Cliffs, N.J.: Prentice Hall.

Duncan, H. D. (1965). *Culture and Democracy*. New York: Bedminster Press.

170

Durkheim, E. (1897; 1951). *Suicide.* Translated by J. A. Spaulding and G. Simpson. Glencoe, Ill.: Free Press.

Etzioni, A. (1993). *The Spirit of Community: Rights, Responsibilities, and the Communitarian Agenda.* New York: Crown.

Felson, M. (1994). *Crime and Everyday Life.* Thousand Oaks, Calif.: Pine Forge Press.

Frei, H. (1992). *Louis Henry Sullivan.* Zurich: Artemis.

Friedman, L. M. (1985). *A History of American Law.* New York: Simon and Schuster.

Garreau, J. (1991). *Edge City: Life on the New Frontier.* New York: Doubleday.

Gordon, P., and H. W. Richardson (1997). Are Compact Cities a Desirable Planning Goal? *Journal of the American Planning Association* 63:95–107. Cambridge, Mass.: Northern Light Technology LLC.

Granovetter, M. S. (1973). The Strength of Weak Ties. *American Journal of Sociology* 78:1360–80.

Gruen Associates (1976). *Notes on the Urban Dynamics of Southern California.* Irvine: University of California Extension Project, October 20.

Jacobs, J. (1961). *The Death and Life of Great American Cities.* New York: Random House.

Jacoby, J. E., ed. (1994). *Classics of Criminology.* Prospect Heights, Ill.: Waveland.

Jencks, C. (1993). *Heteropolis.* London: Ernst and Sohn.

Johnson, J. (1995). Links, Arrows, and Networks: Fundamental Metaphors in Human Thought. In D. Batten, J. Casti, and R. Thord (eds.), *Networks in Action.* Berlin: Springer-Verlag.

Kelling, G. L., and C. M. Coles (1996). *Fixing Broken Windows: Restoring Order and Reducing Crime in Our Communities.* New York: Free Press.

Kessler, D. A. (1993). Integrating Calls for Service with Community- and Problem-Oriented Policing: A Case Study. *Crime and Delinquency* 39:485–508.

Kunstler, J. H. (1993). *The Geography of Nowhere: The Rise and Decline of American's Man-Made Landscape.* New York: Simon and Schuster.

Laszlo, E., R. Artigiani, A. Combs, and V. Csanyi (1996). *Changing Visions: Human Cognitive Maps: Past, Present, and Future.* Westport, Conn.: Praeger.

Liss, J., and S. Schlossman (1984). The Contours of Crime Prevention in

August Vollmer's Berkeley. *Research in Law, Deviance, and Social Control* 6:79–107.

McMillan, B., P. Florin, J. Stevenson, B. Kerman, and R. E. Mitchell (1995). Empowerment Praxis in Community Coalitions. *American Journal of Community Psychology* 23:699–728.

Milgram, S. (1963). Behavioral Study of Obedience. *Journal of Abnormal and Social Psychology* 67:371–78.

——— (1965). Some Conditions of Obedience and Disobedience to Authority. *Human Relations* 18:57–76.

Neal, A. G. (1971). Alienation and Social Control. In J. P. Scott and S. F. Scott (eds.), *Social Control and Social Change*. Chicago: University of Chicago Press.

Newman, O. (1972). *Defensible Space: Crime Prevention through Urban Design*. New York: Macmillan.

Perkins, D. D., B. B. Brown, and R. B. Taylor (1996). The Ecology of Empowerment: Predicting Participation in Community Organizations. *Journal of Social Issues* 52:85–110.

Ross, K. L. (1996). Rights, Responsibilities, and Communitarianism. <http://www.friesian.com/rights.htm>. November 10, 1997.

Rubenstein, H., C. Murray, T. Motoyama, and W. V. Rouse (1980). The Link between Crime and the Built Environment: The Current State of Knowledge. Research brief prepared for the United States Department of Justice, National Institute of Justice.

Sagoff, M. (1997). Do We Consume Too Much? *Atlantic* 279:80–96.

Sampson, R. J. (1991). Linking the Micro- and Macro-Level Dimensions of Community Social Organization. *Social Forces* 70:43–65.

——— (1995). The Community. In J. Q. Wilson and J. Petersilia (eds.), *Crime*. San Francisco: ICS Press.

Sampson, R. J., and J. H. Laub (1993). *Crime in the Making*. Cambridge: Harvard University Press.

Sampson, R. J., S. W. Raudenbush, and F. Earls (1997). Neighborhoods and Violent Crime: A Multilevel Study of Collective Efficacy. *Science* 277:918–24.

Sarkissian, W., A. Forsyth, and H. Warwick (1990). Residential "Social Mix": The Debate Continues. *Australian Planner* 28:5–16.

Schlossman, S. (1983). The Chicago Area Project Revisited. *Crime and Delinquency* 29:398–462.

Skogan, W. G. (1990). *Disorder and Decline*. Berkeley: University of California Press.

Skolnick, J. H., and J. J. Fyfe (1993). *Above the Law: Police and the Excessive Use of Force*. New York: Free Press.

Smith, B. E., and R. C. Davis (1993). Successful Community Anticrime Programs: What Makes Them Work? In R. C. Davis, A. J. Lurigio, and D. P. Rosenbaum (eds.), *Drugs and the Community: Involving Community Residents in Combating the Sale of Illegal Drugs*. Springfield, Ill.: Charles C. Thomas.

Soja, E. (1992). Inside Exopolis: Scenes from Orange County. In M. Sorkin (ed.), *Variations on a Theme Park: The New American City and the End of Public Space*. New York: Hill and Wang.

Spence, K. (1994). Cultural Identity and Democratic Participation. Paper presented at the Citizenship and Cultural Frontiers Conference, Staffordshire University, England, September 16. <http://mail.bris.ac.uk/~pokgs/fntabs.html>. May 16, 1998.

Sullivan, L. H. (1979). *What Is Architecture? Kindergarten Chats and Other Writings*. New York: Dover.

Taylor, R. B. (1997). Social Order and Disorder of Street Blocks and Neighborhoods: Ecology, Microecology, and the Systemic Model of Social Disorganization. *Journal of Research in Crime and Delinquency* 34:113–55.

Trojanowicz, R., and B. Bucqueroux (1990). *Community Policing: A Contemporary Perspective*. Cincinnati: Anderson.

Verba, S., K. Lehman Schlozman, H. Brady, and N. H. Nie (1993). Citizen Activity: Who Participates? What Do They Say? *American Political Science Review* 87:303–18.

Wilson, J. Q. (1970). *Varieties of Police Behavior: The Management of Law and Order in Eight Communities*, 2d ed. New York: Atheneum.

Wilson, J. Q., and G. L. Kelling. (1982). Broken Windows. *Atlantic* 249, no. 3:29–36.

———. (1989). Making Neighborhoods Safe. *Atlantic* 263, no. 2:46–52.

Zimbardo, P. (1969). The Human Choice: Individuation, Reason, and Order versus Deindividuation, Impulse, and Chaos. *Nebraska Symposium on Motivation* 237–307.

——— (1974). On "Obedience to Authority." *American Psychologist* 29:566–67.

Index

Communitarianism *(cont.)*
37; as undermining community,
138–39, 144

Community (Communities, Community-building): alienation and
schism in, by class and race, 17–18,
61, 83, 138, 139; anticrime efforts,
100, 145; capacity to build, 6–7,
24; capacity to build, in low-income
areas, 7–8, 78; consensus and alliances, 46, 54, 70, 84; as contested
concept, 134–35; counterintuitive
logic against, 108; definition of
problems in, 70; desire and need
for, 70, 159; determinants of intervention in, 90; dialogue in, 24, 68,
156; difficulties in building, 11–12,
24, 62, 101, 132; good-neighboring
in, 52, 80, 108; indigenous skills,
35, 50, 58, 68, 158; lack of ties in,
127, 158; malls as symbolically
built around, 80; motivation of leaders, 78; need for alternative views
of, 95, 143; role structure, 32, 52–
53, 105; state and paradox of, 132,
151; strengths, 18, 28, 47, 104,
127–28

Community ecology: balance of, 55;
computer modeling of, 77; fragile
inner-city, 70; as part of whole picture, 67, 82, 123; in relation to cognitive processes, 77; in relation to
crime, 76, 150; stability of, 35, 48,
79, 83, 155

Community policing, 12–13, 25, 56;
and community leaders, 54; defined,
14, 34; and feelings of citizens, 39;
hopes of, 37; nostalgia versus reality, 34–35; officer in, 13; paradox
of, 93–94, 103, 141; problems with,
18, 42, 44, 46–47, 92; role of community in, 13, 35, 43; theory, 45;
ubiquitous nature of, 46, 48

Condé Nast Traveler, 157

Connection(s), 48, 53, 83; establishing,
57, 150; failure to understand, 93,
152; Heritage Park versus Montclair, Calif., 112–14; loss of, 128;

place as central to, 122; in problem
solving, 79, 151; as social control,
123, 125; as social network, 127;
and Starbucks, 109; strengthening
of, 127

Consumption, 80–83, 153; in black
communities, 81; and home buying,
120–21; malls as safe places for, 131

Cooperation. *See* Culture

COP Shops, 55–57, 59, 60–62, 137;
and Neighborhood Action Programs, 61; and NOP (Neighborhood Observation and Patrol), 59,
68; regarding people of color, 63; as
"spy shops," 63, 68; Cheryl Steele
and, 56

Coproduction of safety, 68. *See also*
Community policing; Policing

Crime: and economy, 28–29, 67; factors influencing, 28; fear of, 107,
143, 148, 154–55; in influencing
grassroots leaders, 78; in Irvine,
Calif., 114, in Mukilteo, Wash.,
114; police lack of emotional response to, 40; property, 99; rates,
27, 32, 39, 54; targets, 99

Crime and Everyday Life (Felson), 99

Crime control: as culture's value statement, 27; current conception of, 70,
145; failure to appreciate role of
place in, 85, 105; forms of, 12, 95,
141; limits of current model, 41–42,
46–47, 61, 70, 152; limited views
of, 32, 67, 129; paradox of, 85; as
product of community, 18, 48, 127,
158; roles of citizens in, 48; roles of
leadership in, 30

Crime-mapping, 33, 54. *See also* Geographic boundaries

Crime prevention: Home Alert, 24; limits of, 78; Neighborhood Watch,
24, 100; role of community in, 5, 6

Crime Prevention Through Environmental Design (CPTED), 96, 98,
105; in British Columbia, 98; in Irvine, Calif., 98; in Phoenix, 97

Criminal justice system: and cheapening of democracy, 95, 149; in crime